BOOKS ON SPORTS

For boys and girls, men and women, for all from the beginner to the top professional, for the leisure-time sportsman and for the serious competitor.

More than 100 titles are offered in the following sports:

BASEBALL • BASKETBALL • BOATING • BOWLING • BOXING • CAMPING • CANOEING • CHEERLEADING • FENCING • FIGURE SKATING • FISHING • FOOTBALL • GOLF • HANDBALL • HOCKEY • HORSEBACK RIDING • HUNTING • LACROSSE • PHYSICAL CONDITIONING • ROPING • SAILING • SELF DEFENSE • SKIING • SOCCER • SOFTBALL • SWIMMING AND DIVING • TENNIS • TRACK AND FIELD • TUMBLING • VOLLEYBALL • WRESTLING

The RONALD SPORTS LIBRARY (incorporating the original Barnes Sports Library) is recognized as one of the most complete and widely used lists of sports books available anywhere in the world. The series consists of instructional, how-to books profusely illustrated and brief in length.

The OUTDOOR SPORTSMAN'S LIBRARY is another featured series. Hunters, fishermen, campers, and water sports enthusiasts will find good reading here.

Advanced books are available for the mature sports reader as well as a diversified list of textbooks and reference volumes in the area of physical education.

SPRINGBOARD DIVING

By

PHIL MORIARTY

Head Swimming and Diving Coach
Yale University

Assisted by

CHRISTIAN SPARKS

THE RONALD PRESS COMPANY · NEW YORK

Copyright, ©, 1959, by
THE RONALD PRESS COMPANY

2

Library of Congress Catalog Card Number: 59–15163

PRINTED IN THE UNITED STATES OF AMERICA

Foreword

It is indeed a great privilege, as well as a pleasure, to say a word concerning Philip Moriarty, my long-time colleague and my successor as swimming coach at Yale University, on the occasion of the publication of his book on diving.

Growing up in New Haven, and interested in aquatics early in life, he naturally gravitated toward the Yale swimming program and friendship with the writer; with Harry Burke, the Yale freshman coach and long-time swimming teacher in the New Haven area; and another New Havener, Karl Michael, now head coach of swimming at Dartmouth College, who was then head diving coach and assistant swimming coach at Yale.

Phil Moriarty joined the staff at Yale in 1932, and it was soon discovered he had a great flair for teaching. He was soon given responsibility in diving and swimming on the varsity level.

When Karl Michael left Yale, in the fall of 1939, to accept the post as head swimming and diving coach at Dartmouth, Phil accepted the offer at Yale as instructor in physical education, assistant swimming coach, and head diving coach. On July 1, 1959, he was appointed head coach of swimming and diving, along with his post in physical education.

Phil Moriarty has had full and rich experience as a member of the Yale staff, being responsible for conducting many outstanding swimming meets, such as the Eastern Intercollegiate Swimming League Championships, the National Collegiate Athletic Association Championships, and National Amateur Athletic Union Indoor Swimming Championships; and he has conducted clinics for the State Department in Iceland, India, Ceylon, and Cambodia.

He is held in high esteem in the administrative field, as evidenced by his presidency of the Connecticut Association of the A.A.U., his national chairmanship of the A.A.U. Men's Swimming Records Com-

iii

mittee; his chairmanship of the N.C.A.A. Swimming Rules Committee; and membership on the Executive Committee of the Conference for National Cooperation in Aquatics (CNCA).

However, I consider his greatest asset to be his outstanding ability as a teacher; quiet, yet firm; analytical, and with it all, having the ability to inspire the pupil. Through the years, I have been impressed by the fact that almost all the outstanding divers of the United States (which means the outstanding divers of the world) have sought him out for coaching. At championship meets he is always surrounded by the champions, as well as the young aspiring divers, seeking information, advice, and his invaluable and patient counsel. On a number of occasions, the Olympic Games aspirants who later became Olympic champions have spent the pre-Games period training with him.

I know of no one better qualified to do a book on diving which will be valuable to the beginner as well as to the champion, for I have been in a position, these past thirty years, to know and evaluate Phil Moriarty as a great teacher as well as a great influence in the lives of young men and women. This practical book literally makes Phil Moriarty's coaching available to every reader.

Robert J. H. Kiphuth
PROFESSOR OF PHYSICAL EDUCATION AND
HEAD COACH OF SWIMMING, EMERITUS,
YALE UNIVERSITY
UNITED STATES OLYMPIC SWIMMING COACH,
1928, 1932, 1936, 1940, and 1948

Preface

This book is primarily intended for the beginner in diving. It is hoped also that it will prove useful both to those who have some diving skills and to diving coaches themselves. But no previous knowledge of or achievement in diving is presupposed of the reader.

Undoubtedly there are many people who would like to be able to dive but who have no method of obtaining competent instruction. *Springboard Diving* aims to make such instruction easily available to all.

United States divers have excelled in international competition ever since 1920, yet it is strongly felt that the caliber of performance of the average diver is poor. The main reason for this is the shortage of coaches who are familiar with good diving. Basically, anyone with a sound body and a desire to learn can become a good diver—*if properly schooled.* This is not to say that everyone can be a champion, far from it; the rewards of diving, as in many other sports, are chiefly the pleasure and satisfaction that come of doing something as well as you can. Unfortunately, the young enthusiast of today often has nowhere to turn for help in his or her desire to be a proficient diver.

This book has been planned to give the diving novice the help he needs. It provides a chapter by chapter description and a clear-cut analysis of the basic, and later of some of the more complex, dives. Terms which may be unfamiliar to the beginner are carefully defined. And answers will readily be found to questions about technique and "know-how." Thus there can be secured a sound foundation in the basic principles of diving and a knowledge of the movements which, with practice, will enable a diver to perform the most complicated dives.

Springboard diving is a sport that involves such highly coordinated activity that it is impractical to describe in words alone the multiple processes involved in the execution of a dive. For this reason a means has been provided whereby an over-all pictorial impression could be gained of the *dive in action*. This means is the sequence series. Each of the twelve sequence series contains twenty photographs showing the many integrated movements that compose a correctly performed dive. Simply by flipping these photographs, an excellent and accurate idea can be gained of what the dive actually looks like. An additional advantage of the sequence series is that each movement of a dive may be studied individually, together with the brief descriptive comment which is provided for every photo.

Springboard Diving will prove especially instructive when studied and used by two people together. Father and son, mother and daughter, any two friends, can help each other, with the help of the sequence series, toward better and more enjoyable diving. Individual divers, diving competitors, and coaches should also find it a highly useful means of improving standards of performance. In short, the information, guidance, and encouragement thus given should actively assist in the development of skills and greatly add to the enjoyment of participating in the sport of diving.

I express my gratitude to Chris Sparks, a swimming and diving coach in his own right, for the flip-picture idea, for the introduction and history, and for his able assistance in the preparation of this book. Grateful acknowledgment is made to Bob Clotworthy, former Olympic Diving Gold Medalist and now Head Swimming and Diving Coach at Princeton University, who specially demonstrated the divers pictured in the sequence series. Thanks are also due to Miss Fran Wilson, who posed for several of the illustrations in the text, and to Manuel Sylvia, Head of the Department of Fine Arts at Wilbur Cross High School, and Oscar Kiphuth, Assistant Professor, Yale University, for their help in developing and processing the photographs.

PHIL MORIARTY

New Haven, Connecticut
August, 1959

Contents

Contents

SPRINGBOARD DIVING

I: INTRODUCTION

1. How Diving Developed

Almost certainly the first instruction on swimming techniques printed in the English language was *Master Digbie's Book of the Art of Swimming*, published in a translation from the Latin in 1595. In a paragraph entitled "To Dive Underneath the Water," Master Digbie describes what the diver must do: "He must, if he be in a place where he may stand upon the ground, with as much force as he can, leap up, and bending his head towards his breast fall forwards downe into the water. . . . His hands he must holde before his head, with their backs together. . . ." The purpose in keeping the backs, rather than the palms, of the hands together was to enable the diver to pull himself down after breaking the surface, "forcing him downe under the water." There was no such thing as a springboard in 1595. However, the remainder of Digbie's description could serve, even today, as a fairly accurate guide to the most elementary form of dive—a good means of getting into the water quickly, but scarcely a sport.

Diving as we know it in competition today is actually of comparatively recent origin. There may well have been early diving contests, as there were other contests of skill, strength, or endurance. But it was not until the latter part of the nineteenth century, when German and Swedish acrobats and gymnasts started to move to the swimming area to perform their tumbling routines, that acrobatic or "fancy" diving developed. "Plain" diving from a fixed platform became part of the swimming program when the Olympic Games were revived at the beginning of the twentieth century. By 1908, however, in the fourth modern Olympiad held in London, there was a full program of "fancy diving." The Olympic Committee of the day composed a table which listed the types of dive allowed, descriptions of them, and a value for each dive based on the difficulty of performance.

3

This early table listed a mere fourteen dives from the high platform and twenty dives from the springboard, as compared today to forty-two dives and fifty dives, respectively.

The dives which were performed in those early days were simple movements and rarely combined intricate twists and multiple somer-

Dive No.	Dive	Degree of Difficulty					
		1 METER DIVE			3 METER DIVE		
		Tuck	Pike	Layout	Tuck	Pike	Layout
I	**FORWARD DIVES**						
100	Forward Dive	1.2	1.3	1.4	1.3	1.4	1.6
101	Forward Somersault	1.6	1.6	1.8	1.7	1.7	1.8
102	Forward 1½ Somersault	1.6	1.7	—	1.6	1.6	2.1
103	Forward Double Somersault	2.1	2.2	—	2.1	2.2	—
104	Forward 2½ Somersault	2.2	2.4	—	2.1	2.3	—
105	Forward Triple Somersault	—	—	—	2.6	—	—
106	Forward 3½ Somersault	—	—	—	2.7	—	—
111	Flying Forward Somersault	1.5	1.7	—	1.6	1.7	—
112	Flying Forward 1½ Somersault	1.8	1.9	—	1.7	1.8	—
II	**BACK DIVES**						
200	Back Dive	1.6	1.6	1.6	1.7	1.7	1.7
201	Back Somersault	1.5	1.6	1.7	1.5	1.7	1.6
202	Back 1½ Somersault	2.2	2.3	2.4	2.0	2.2	2.2
203	Back Double Somersault	2.2	2.3	—	2.0	2.2	2.4
204	Back 2½ Somersault	—	—	—	2.7	—	—
211	Flying Back Somersault	1.7	—	—	1.6	—	—
212	Flying Back 1½ Somersault	—	—	—	2.1	—	—
III	**REVERSE DIVES**						
300	Reverse Dive	1.7	1.7	1.7	1.7	1.9	1.9
301	Reverse Somersault	1.4	1.8	2.0	1.5	1.7	1.9
302	Reverse 1½ Somersault	2.2	2.4	—	2.2	2.4	2.6
303	Reverse Double Somersault	2.2	—	—	2.2	2.4	—
304	Reverse 2½ Somersault	—	—	—	2.8	—	—
311	Flying Reverse Somersault	1.7	—	—	1.6	—	—
312	Flying Reverse 1½ Somersault	—	—	—	2.4	—	—
IV	**INWARD DIVES**						
400	Inward Dive	1.2	1.3	1.7	1.2	1.3	1.5
401	Inward Somersault	1.7	1.9	—	1.5	1.7	—

Table of Dives and Degree of Difficulty Factors

From the 1959 Official A.A.U. Swimming Guide, designed by Jack Smith.

saults. In the report of the fourth Olympiad, mention was made of a diver who spoiled his chances of winning by attempting to execute a forward double somersault. The report went on to suggest that this dive be eliminated from future programs because it was believed that no diver could control the execution of so many spins without serious

Dive No.	Dive	Degree of Difficulty					
		1 METER DIVE			3 METER DIVE		
		Tuck	Pike	Layout	Tuck	Pike	Layout
IV	**INWARD DIVES (Cont.)**						
402	Inward 1½ Somersault	2.2	2.4	—	2.0	2.2	—
403	Inward Double Somersault	—	—	—	2.3	2.4	—
404	Inward 2½ Somersault	—	—	—	2.6	—	—
411	Flying Inward Somersault	—	—	—	1.8	—	—
V	**TWIST DIVES**						
510	Forward Dive ½ Twist	—	1.7	1.8	—	1.8	1.9
511	Forward Dive 1 Twist	—	2.1	2.0	—	2.1	2.0
512	Forward Somersault ½ Twist	—	1.5	1.8	—	1.7	1.9
513	Forward Somersault 1 Twist	—	2.0	—	—	2.0	—
514	Forward 1½ Somersault ½ Twist	2.0	2.1	—	1.9	2.0	—
515	Forward 1½ Somersault 1 Twist	—	2.2	—	—	2.1	—
516	Forward 1½ Somersault Double Twist	—	2.7	—	—	2.4	—
520	Back Dive ½ Twist	—	2.0	1.7	—	1.9	1.6
521	Back Dive 1 Twist	—	—	2.1	—	—	2.0
522	Back Somersault ½ Twist	—	1.7	1.7	—	1.8	1.8
523	Back Somersault 1 Twist	—	1.9	—	—	2.0	2.0
524	Back Somersault 1½ Twist	—	2.1	—	—	2.1	2.1
525	Back Dive ½ Twist 1½ Somersault	2.2	2.3	—	2.0	2.1	—
526	Back 1½ Somersault 1½ Twist	—	2.6	—	—	2.4	—
527	Back 1½ Somersault 2½ Twist	—	—	—	—	2.7	—
530	Reverse Dive ½ Twist	—	2.2	1.9	—	2.2	2.0
531	Reverse Dive 1 Twist	—	—	2.3	—	—	2.2
532	Reverse Dive ½ Twist & Somersault	1.9	2.0	—	2.0	2.1	—
533	Reverse Somersault 1 Twist	2.3	2.3	2.3	2.2	2.2	2.2
534	Reverse Somersault 1½ Twist	2.1	2.1	—	—	2.2	2.2
535	Reverse Dive ½ Twist 1½ Somersault	2.1	2.2	—	—	2.1	—
536	Reverse 1½ Somersault 1½ Twist	—	2.7	—	—	2.6	—
540	Inward Dive ½ Twist	—	1.8	2.1	—	1.8	2.0
541	Inward Dive 1 Twist	—	—	—	—	2.2	2.2
542	Inward Somersault ½ Twist	1.9	1.9	—	2.0	2.0	—

Agreed Upon by F.I.N.A., N.C.A.A., and N.A.A.U.

risk of injury. Today divers spin forward three and one-half times with perfect accuracy, and perform double twisting forward one-and-one-half somersaults and other dives equally complicated.

The diving lists and tables have been in a constant state of change ever since their beginnings. Obsolete dives have been dropped or changed; new dives have been added. A milestone in diving progress was reached in 1929 when dives were divided into five groups, which are technically the same today: forward, backward, reverse, inward, and twisting. For platform dives there are six groups, the additional classification being handstand dives.

The names of the dives themselves have also been changed through the years. In the early days a dive was often named after its originator. Islander and Molberg were Swedish divers whose names were linked to dives in this way. Islander's Dive is called the Reverse Dive today, although it has also been known by several other names: Overback, Half-turn; Flying Dutchman; and Half Gainer. Molberg's Dive, now the Reverse Somersault, has been known as the Overback, One Turn; Flying Dutchman Somersault; and Full Gainer. A glance at the list of present-day dives (pages 4 and 5) will give you a good idea of how comparatively simple and descriptive the terminology of dives is today.

Beginning with the Olympic Games of 1920 (which excluded German athletes), United States divers have dominated international competitive diving. A large part of this supremacy can perhaps be credited to two great coaches on the American scene: Ernst Brandsten, an outstanding Swedish diver in the 1912 games, and Fred Cady, a sportsminded artist. Brandsten's great contribution was his thoroughness in teaching fundamentals and his success in standardizing equipment. Fred Cady's influence on the development of diving derived from his artistic awareness of grace and poise. The ideas and teaching methods that these two men contributed, and the tradition of diving excellence which stemmed from them, helped to produce U.S. diving champions in all the Olympic Games since 1920.

Diving has seen many great developments since the beginning of this century. Not only are there now many more dives to be performed, but they are in many cases infinitely more complex than was believed possible fifty years ago. New techniques are constantly being developed and adapted. (Even the springboard itself, always wooden until after World War II, is now frequently made of aluminum, plastic, or fiberglass.) Whereas fifty years ago diving was only beginning to make an impact as a sport, today it is one of the most vital and fascinating branches of aquatics.

2. What Every Beginner Should Know

Sometimes in the following chapters you will come across the phrase "the rules require." You may well ask, "Who makes these rules?" The aim of the present chapter is to answer this question and other questions which will occur to every beginner. For instance: How is diving organized? What is "degree of difficulty"? What is a "basic dive"? When can I enter a contest? What does a judge look for? Is there such a thing as a perfect dive? Is diving dangerous?

The two organizations which govern swimming and diving in the United States are the National Collegiate Athletic Association (N.C.A.A.) and the National Amateur Athletic Union (N.A.A.U.). The first organization controls all competition for college and interscholastic athletics; the second controls the competition for all amateurs, including collegians, when they are competing in open meets. The N.C.A.A. and the N.A.A.U. cooperate in rule-making, and both publish Swimming Guides which list dives and their *degrees of difficulty*. Each dive has a certain difficulty value based on a point system. Thus, the simplest dives in the book (the Forward Dive Tuck, for instance) are rated at 1.2, while the most difficult dive (the Reverse Two-and-one-half Somersault) carries a degree of difficulty of 2.8. (See pages 4 and 5 for a complete list of dives and their difficulty ratings.) The degree of difficulty is determined by committee accord —though of course the committee does not originate dives. New dives come about through the imagination and daring of divers themselves.

There were fifty-four dives listed in the diving table in 1958. (The number varies as new dives are added and old ones are dropped.) These dives are divided into five *basic groups:* forward, backward, reverse, inward, and twisting. These terms refer to the difference in the *direction* of a dive. Two dives may be closely related to one another—in technique, fundamental movement, position, skills required —and yet, because of the basic difference of direction, the two may well be in different groups.

Most of the dives listed in the table can be performed in two positions, and some in three. The three possible positions are (1) layout, (2) pike, and (3) tuck. The accompanying illustrations will give you a better idea of these positions than words can.*

Layout Position   **Pike Position**   **Tuck Position**

Rules have varied through the years as to which dives must be performed by divers as their *required,* or obligatory, dives in dual meets or championship contests. Usually the *required dives* are the first dive in each basic group: the Forward Dive, the Back Dive, the Reverse Dive, the Inward Dive, and the Forward Dive One-half Twist. Hence these are often known as *basic dives.* Besides these five dives, the divers also have to perform *optional dives,* one selected from each of the basic groups.

As in boxing or figure skating, the winner of a diving contest is determined by the opinion of the judges, who are familiar with diving from observation or former participation. They must, of course, know all the rules governing the execution of a dive. The parts of the dive that the judges consider are the run, the takeoff, technique and grace of movement during passage through the air, and the entry into the water. For example, in a dive performed in the pike position, the judge will look carefully to see whether the pike is bent deeply at

---

* See also the Glossary of Diving Terms (page 53) for definition of any technical term used in the book.

the waist, whether the legs are held straight at the knees, and whether the toes are properly pointed.

There are always three judges for a dual meet, and either five or seven judges for a championship contest. After observing a dive in all its intricate parts, each judge makes his award without consulting the other judges. He will score the dive (in any contest) on a scale from ten, for a very good dive, down to zero, for a failed dive. The awards of the judges are then added together. (When more than three judges are used, the highest score and the lowest score are dropped out and only the remaining three or five scores are used.) This total is then multiplied by the degree of difficulty, and the result is the final award. Let's illustrate this with a practical example: A diver in a championship contest with five judges performs as one of his optional dives the Inward One-and-one-half Somersault in the tuck position. From the one-meter board this dive has a degree of difficulty of 2.2. The five judges score him as follows: 7, 8, 5, 7, 6. To calculate the final award, first drop out the 8 and the 5 (the highest and the lowest score); then add the other three scores and multiply 20 (the total) by 2.2 (the degree of difficulty). The diver's final score on this dive is 44.0.

Since at least three opinions enter into the judgment of a dive, a final award of a "perfect ten" is rare. In nearly thirty years connected with diving, I have only seen one case where all the judges awarded ten for a dive. This was in the 1932 Men's Senior Indoor A.A.U. Championship held at Yale University. Dick Degner, the great Michigan diver and Olympic champion, performed a Reverse One-and-one-half Somersault Pike which was scored at ten by all seven judges. If there are "perfect" dives, this was certainly one of them. For practical purposes, perfection is almost impossible to expect in a dive—but it is always worth striving for. Actually, any increase in score will give you a great sense of achievement and satisfaction, as does all improvement.

Before we begin, perhaps it is necessary to say a word about the so-called "dangers" of diving. Diving is, in fact, very far from being a dangerous sport. Compared to injuries received in football, skiing, riding, baseball, and many other sports, those sustained in diving are few and are not severe. Making a flat entry into the water, for instance, is not dangerous, and the pain associated with it is usually greatly exaggerated.

Injuries are caused either by faulty technique or by poor equipment. Faulty technique can be eliminated by practice and by a proper understanding of the mechanics of a dive. And observation of the rules governing equipment will ensure maximum safety in the physical environment of the dive. (See pages 10 and 11 and the table below for the setup of the boards and pool.) Regulations governing the surface of the board and the amount of elevation, requirements that the diving end of the board shall be above the fixed end, and the rule that readily adjustable fulcrums should be used—all contribute to making diving a more thoroughly safe sport.

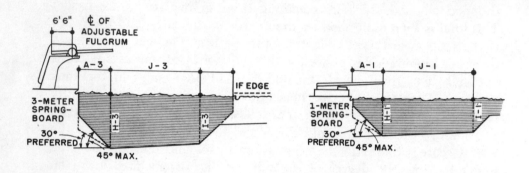

Type of Board†	Length	Width	Height Above Water	DISTANCES*									
				From Edge of Pool to End of Board		From Center of Board to Side of Pool		From Center of Board to Center of Next Board		From End of Board to Wall Ahead		From Board to Beam on Ceiling Above	
1-Meter Springboard	16'	20"	3' 3"	A-1	7'-5'	B-1	10'-8'	C-1	8'-6'	D-1	28'-25'	E-1	15'
3-Meter Springboard	16'	20"	9' 11"	A-3	7'-5'	B-3	15'-12'	C-3	10'-8'	D-3	33'-30'	E-3	15'
5-Meter Platform	18'	7'	16' 5"	A-5	7'-5'	B-5	15'-12'	C-5	10'-8'	D-5	43'-35'	E-5	15'
10-Meter Platform	20'	8' 10'	32' 10"	A-10	8'-5'	B-10	20'-15'	C-10	10'-8'	D-10	52'-45'	E-10	15'-12'

* Where two figures are given, the first is the preferred dimension and the second is the minimum safe dimension. † The 7-meter platform is shown in the diagram for general information only. It is not an official diving height, but is recommended and is frequently built as an intermediate teaching level between the official 5- and 10-meter

Section of a Swimming Pool, with Springboards
(Used by permission of R. Jackson Smith,

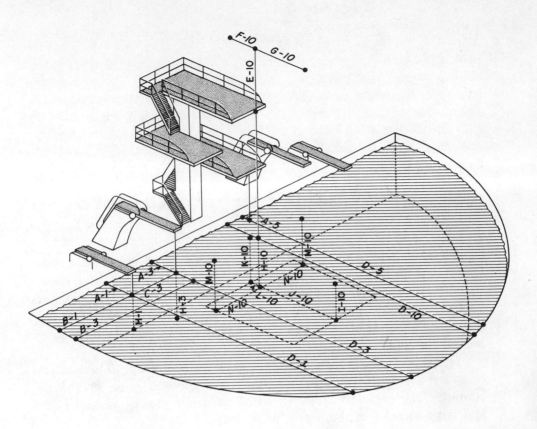

Clear Overhead Behind End of Board	Clear Overhead Ahead of Board	Below End of Board	WATER DEPTHS*					
			AT VARYING DISTANCES FROM END OF BOARD					
			Depth	Distance in Front	Depth	Distance in Back	Depth	Distance Each Side
F-1 6'-5'	G-1 15'-12'	H-1 11'-10'	I-1 9'	J-1 17'	K-1 9'	L-1 3'	M-1 9'	N-1 8'
F-3 6'-5'	G-3 15'-12'	H-3 12'-11½'	I-3 10'	J-3 20'	K-3 9'	L-3 3'	M-3 10'	N-3 10'
F-5 8'-6'	G-5 15'-12'	H-5 14'-12½'	I-5 11'	J-5 25'	K-5 9'	L-5 3'	M-5 11'	N-5 10'
F-10 8'-6'	G-10 15'-12'	H-10 16'-15'	I-10 14'	J-10 35'	K-10 10'	L-10 3'	M-10 14'	N-10 10'

platforms. The 7-meter platform should compare in size with the 5-meter platform, and depths of water should comply with depths for the 10-meter platform.

All diving facilities should be built to correct heights above the water, with a maximum tolerance of 5 per cent permissible where water level or indoor ceiling conditions make a deviation necessary.

and Platforms, and Table of Distances and Depths.

Eggers and Higgins, Architects, New York.)

11

3. Warm-up Exercises

Before any athletic contest or practice session it is necessary for the athlete to "warm up" in order to loosen the muscles and allow the organs of the body to adjust to increased action. The runner jogs around the track, the football player performs calisthenics, the fencer does leg stretching exercises, and the swimmer swims many laps of the pool.

The diver has his own special way of warming up. These exercises are simple to perform but vital to a good practice session or contest. One typical warm-up routine to loosen the trunk and back and large muscles of the legs is as follows:

Do deep knee bends. (Ten times.)

Bend trunk and touch toes from standing position. (Ten times.)

Sit on a flat surface with legs stretched out in front and toes pointed. Grasp the back of the knees and bend trunk forward, touching the thighs with the chest and placing the forehead on the knees. (Ten times.)

Stand in a straddle position, raise arms overhead, and bend laterally, first right and then left, keeping head between upstretched arms. (Five times right, five times left.)

Ankle stretching and toe pointing are also of great importance to the diver. Here are two suggested exercises:

Sitting on a bench, rest the left ankle on the right knee. Place both hands, palms down, on the top of the left instep and pull hard, rolling the toes under. This should be done several times with each foot.

12

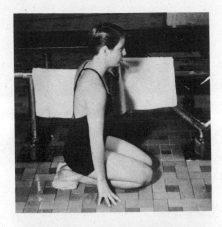

Kneel on the floor with legs together, ankles and toes fully extended. A pad, such as a rolled towel, should be placed beneath the feet for protection. From this position sit back, resting most of your weight on the heels, and bounce up and down. Try to keep your ankles together to permit a full stretch of the foot.

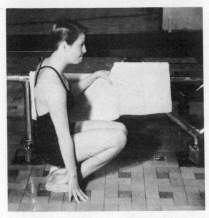

Extreme stretching can be accomplished by lifting both knees off the floor and shifting all your weight back over the ankles and toes. In your first few workouts this exercise should be approached with caution to avoid overextension.

After these preliminary exercises, you will be ready to run through a series of forward and backward approaches (see pages 15-18 and 23-25.) In making an approach avoid continuous bouncing of the board. This is poor practice for many reasons. It often leads to injury, for you may slip and twist an ankle or give yourself a case of shin splints, which is painful and could keep you out of action for several days. Actually, excessive bouncing of the board is unnecessary because it does not produce a skill that can be used in a contest. Instead, you should practice the complete forward approach with one full lift, return to starting position, and repeat three or four times before beginning the first dive.

Practicing the backward takeoff should be made in the same manner. That is, place yourself in starting position on the end of the board and then spring upward, landing forward on the board about one foot from the end. Avoid continuous bouncing from this position also.

II: FORWARD DIVES

4. Forward Approach

The forward approach comprises all of the following movements or stages, each of which is described in this section: the three-step run toward the end of the board (though technically termed a "run," this movement is usually done at a walking gait); the hurdle (the jump to the end of the board after the run); the ride down (the action of bending the board down); and the press (the final thrust from the board into the dive).

In the execution of forward dives you must always perform the approach to the end of the board. Because your approach can be the key to your success or failure as a diver, this part of springboard diving is the most important fundamental you must learn. *Balance* during this walk and jump on the springboard is essential in giving you the necessary lift into the dive. Without balance and coordination during the approach your chances of making a good dive are slim. To attain effective balance you must coordinate your walk to include proper arm swing and leg thrust into the hurdle. The arm action adds to the force that drives you up into the hurdle, and as you drop to the end of the board you must continue to use your arms properly to maintain balance. Then you must coordinate your movements with those of the board as it is pressed downward. The drive of your legs and your arm-swing upward, perfectly coordinated, will power your lift. A readily adjustable fulcrum, a standard item of equipment, permits you to adjust the board to your natural action, which will aid you in coordinating your movements and those of the board.

Of all the points to remember in executing the approach, none is more important than keeping your eyes focused on the end of the board. Looking away from this point is a common error which contributes to faulty dives. Throughout the complete approach you must watch the end of the board until you are sure that your feet will land squarely on the end.

To plot your approach, first stand with your back to the water, heels flush with the diving end of the board. Then walk four normal steps forward. Stop. Move forward approximately ten inches more. You will now be at a position on the board that should be correct for the beginning of your three-step run.

The first step forward is taken on the foot that you wish to hurdle from, and the first and second steps are of normal walking length. The third step is slightly longer. These steps should be taken with increasing force and speed so that the hurdle jump will carry you upward twelve to fifteen inches and about two or three feet forward, depending on the size and strength of your body. (These figures apply to a person weighing 115 pounds or more.) Pace off the steps several times, adjusting the speed and distance of each. If these steps are taken too quickly you will lean forward over the water before the ride down and press are complete.

The preceding discussion should make you aware of the importance of the movements in the forward approach. Now you must practice and learn to integrate them into your own individual skill.

Before moving into the approach, you should stand in a position of attention for a few seconds. During this brief period you can ready yourself to perform the dive and, in a contest, attract the attention of the judges. Your eyes should be focused on the end of the board and remain there throughout the run and hurdle.

The movement of the arms on the first two steps of a three-step approach should be your normal arm swing as in walking, or any movement that feels natural. The third step must be made with enough ankle, knee, and hip flexion to provide sufficient force to drive the body erect to the highest controlled elevation without strain when the leg is extended. It is in this step that the arms must be brought into simultaneous action so that they swing upward at the same time that you lift your body into the hurdle.

As the takeoff foot is pushing against the board for the hurdle, begin to raise the other leg to form a right angle between the trunk and thigh and also at the back of the knee. The ankle should be in full extension and toes pointed toward the board. While the free leg is rising to this position, the arms are being swung side-upward, elbows straight, to a point well above the head. The combination of pressing one foot against the board and lifting the arms and free leg raises the body high enough for a fully balanced hurdle. As mentioned before, this hurdle should be approximately two to three feet in length and 12 to 15 inches in height.

At the apex of the hurdle begin to straighten the bent leg, so that as you drop to the end of the board the legs come together straight at the knees, with the ankles extended and the toes pointed. During this descent the arms are brought downward in the lateral plane with the body, without too much backward swing from the shoulders. The drop to the board is made in a near-vertical plane for most dives.

The first contact is made with the balls of the feet. Then, as you continue the forceful downward movement of the arms and flex your knees, the heels come in light contact with the board. When the arms reach the bottom of their swing and the knees are deeply bent, begin to swing the arms upward and straighten your legs to drive the board down to its greatest depth. The continuing upward swing of the arms will aid in the lift of your body as the board starts its upward recovery to thrust you into the dive.

The approach should be practiced until you can do it with natural ease. It must be smooth and graceful and at the same time have sufficient force and balance to accomplish its purpose.

If you are having difficulties in developing your forward approach, your errors will probably be one or more of those described below. Any one of these errors can retard your progress and, if not corrected early in your training, will become increasingly difficult to eliminate.

The first of these common errors is rushing the approach to the end of the board. Very often a diver will misunderstand the word "run" in the rule governing the forward approach and will move too quickly toward his hurdle step. This excessive speed will cause a force that cannot be eliminated during the hurdle, and the dive will be pushed outward too great a distance from the end of the board. Most of the better divers have developed a walk (rather than a run) which enables them to maintain good balance and control during the hurdle and takeoff. Follow their technique and develop smooth, slow, and well-balanced steps before the hurdle.

A second error is caused by too much arm swing during the approach. Since your arm action contributes balance and force to your hurdle and takeoff, any unnecessary movements prior to the hurdle should not be used. The arms should swing upward as you start the press into your hurdle, and may reach a point well above your head, but be sure that they are equal in force and not out of phase with your pressing leg. The movement of the arms can create perfect balance, but if not properly coordinated into the whole approach, the arm action can be a complete loss, and a detriment to the dive.

Stomping the board is very often the cause of a poor dive. This error is caused by pushing at the end of the board before it is bent naturally under your weight. If you are too anxious to spring, you bend your knees too soon and kick at the board, causing an uneven oscillation. The rhythm of the board will not be coordinated with your action. You must not apply the drive from your legs until the board is giving you the thrust upward. You will sense this coordination when it is present, and notice quickly when it is not. It is this part of the approach that is referred to when a diver states, "I am catching the board well," or "I can't catch the board." Adjusting the fulcrum can effect a better rhythm between you and the board.

The fourth error is bending forward from the waist while riding the board down through its bending action. Anticipation of the movements required to do the dive is often the cause of this early bending. This error is by far the easiest to correct. Be sure to look at the end of the board throughout your complete approach and hurdle. As you take your jump up into the hurdle, your lifting leg should rise up so the thigh is at right angles to the trunk and parallel to the board. Keep a straight back perpendicular to the board at all times and the bending error will not occur.

5. Forward Dive (Pike)

The Forward Dive Pike, often called the Front Jackknife, is likely to be the first dive you will try. Your first attempt will probably be a plain header, with a quick slap on the thighs with the hands and into the water—and this technique is sure to have been the one first used by many of our great champions. A few simple directions will enable you to learn to do this dive correctly.

The approach to the end of the board is standard for forward dives (pages 15-18). After a perfect drop from the hurdle to the end of the board, keep your body erect as you complete the press and allow the thrust from the board to drive the whole body straight upward. The arms should swing upward in front of you to a point above your head, and you should begin to bend at the hips almost immediately after leaving the board. (Once the feet have left the board, hip flexion or any other movement, such as tucking or piking, cannot affect the elevation of the dive; the force has been established and cannot be diminished by changing position.) As the hips continue to rise, bring the arms gently down toward the legs in preparation for closing the pike. While the maximum lift is being reached, the legs will have a tendency to swing backward because of the early bending at the hips. Avoid this error by drawing the legs forward with the muscles of the abdomen and holding them perpendicular to the water until the hands have made contact with the top of the instep.

The closing of the body to pike position should be complete at the top of the lift, and the opening will start at a point when the head and upper body are pointing straight at the water. The rotation of the whole body should be slight throughout this dive; control it by holding back the leg swing as described, and by a soft, gentle hip flexion into the pike.

The pike is opened for the drop to the water by allowing the legs to swing upward and back after the complete pike is made. The execution of this phase of the dive is made simple by the rotation of the whole body. As the legs swing back to align with the trunk, bring the arms forward and stretch them overhead. The hands should come together and the whole body should be in perfect alignment for a perpendicular entry into the water. During the complete dive you must hold the legs straight at the knees and keep the toes pointed.

6. Forward Dive (Layout)

In learning the Forward Dive Layout it is most important to understand the correct position for the head, arms, and body. A simple exercise will help you get the feel of this position. Lie face down on the diving board with your head toward the diving end. From this position lift the arms, head, and chest off the board so that you are looking at the opposite end of the pool, with your chin not more than eight inches above the board. Straighten the arms out to the side, slightly forward of a line through the shoulders. Then contract the large muscles of the lower back and buttocks to raise the legs slightly off the board, and point the toes. To avoid excessive arching of the back, this leg elevation should not be more than six inches at the top of the instep. The complete exercise should be done over and over again until you can feel exactly which muscles control this position. Check with your coach or other divers with whom you may be working to see that the position you are assuming is the same as that shown here.

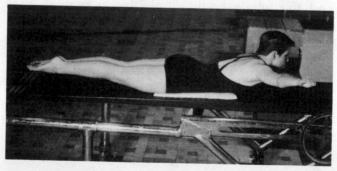

When you have the feel of the layout position, and have mastered the forward approach so that you can consistently land on the end of the board straight up and down for a good takeoff position, you will be ready to start the mechanics of this dive. After riding the board down, you should swing your arms up into the spread position slightly over your head, and as you leave the board, lift the head and chest and arch the back. If this is done properly the legs will begin to lift high up in back, causing your body to rotate and finally pointing you head first toward the water. It is important to avoid making any forward bend at the waist as you leave the board. This error will cause a low rotation point and allow your legs to climb too fast, turning your body over before you have shown a complete layout position and lessening the chances for a vertical entry.

After you attempt this dive once or twice you will be able to decide where the rotation point should be. If the dive turns over too fast, you must consider raising the point of rotation. If the dive hangs or rotates too slowly, you must lower the point of rotation.

During the entire dive you should have your eyes open so that you will be aware of your position with relation to the surface of the water. As you rotate toward the water you should pick out the spot at which you intend to enter. When the body is in a near-vertical position, the arms are brought together overhead. Then the head is dropped forward in line with the upper body, the back is flattened, and the diver enters the water in the perpendicular. Remember at all times that the knees should be straight and the toes pointed for a clean entry. In order to get the maximum award for your effort you must aim for complete ease and a graceful flight through the air, eliminating all jerky or sudden movements. You should also avoid any great lower back arch, often referred to as a "belly-bend." This arch is difficult to remove when you attempt to line up for your entry; and even when you enter the water in the perpendicular, an arched back will very often cause the feet to overthrow, raising a splash.

III: BACK DIVES

7. Backward Takeoff

Balance, coordination, and poise are just as important in the backward dives as in the running forward dives. To attain these skills, good posture is the first essential. Good posture may be defined as good alignment of the skeletal system and control of the muscle groups. Using a mirror for a full view of the body in standing position will be a great advantage in correcting faulty posture.

In performing a backward dive you should first take the same position on the diving board that you would take to begin a forward approach. Stand at attention for a brief moment, walk to the diving end, turn around, and assume a good standing position. The main directive in the rule governing starting position for backward standing dives concerns the arms, which must be extended straight forward from the shoulders. With the arms in this position, set the ball of one foot to rest comfortably on the end of the board and then move the other foot into similar position. Either parallel or angular placement of the feet is correct. For parallel placement, a recommended separation between the feet is one to two inches. In the angular stance, the heels are quite close together and the toes apart, making an inside angle of approximately 30 degrees.

The next combination of movements must give you enough thrust from the board to perform any desired dive. From the balanced starting position most divers use the accepted mannerism of lowering the arms slowly to the sides and then pausing for a few seconds before setting the board in motion. There are two standard methods of setting the board in motion: the three-movement technique, and the four-movement technique. Both methods are sound mechanically, and they will give approximately the same amount of lift. Since the three-movement technique is less complicated it should be tried first.

The Three-movement Technique. It will be to your advantage to know what action the board will follow as you make the three movements for your first backward takeoff. As you pause on the end of the board, heels level with the board and arms at your sides, the first movement is begun by lifting your arms side-upward to a point slightly above your head and pressing up onto your toes. The board will be forced downward. It makes its upward recovery as you swing your arms down hard and flex your knees (second movement). When your arms reach their lowest point, swing them upward again slightly in front of your body as your knees start to straighten. This third action depresses the board to a deep bend which will give you a tremendous thrust upward. The movements of your arms and legs produce a rhythm in the board which, with proper coordination, will spring you high into your dive. For maximum lift you must have full ankle extension and pointed toes as you leave the board. The follow-through of the arm-swing upward during the takeoff gives balance and direction to the dive.

The Four-movement Technique. In the four-movement technique of setting the board in motion, there is one movement which precedes the three described above. In this method you balance on your toes on the end of the board, and after lowering your arms and pausing, the first movement is made by dropping the heels. This will cause a slight movement of the board upward, the opposite of the direction of the first board movement when the three-movement technique is used. All your actions and the actions of the board after this initial move are the same as in the first technique. The additional movement may give some greater lift because the board will move through a greater arc in the next three steps, but if poorly done this technique is apt to cause a loss of balance and direction in the dive.

If you remain in good balance and coordinate your actions with the movements of the board, either of these techniques will result in a good lift, and a good lift gives a better chance of a good dive.

A dive from a backward takeoff is often spoiled by one or more of four common errors. The first of these errors is leaning backward from the end of the board. This leaning is caused by lifting the arms too high and then allowing them to swing down behind the hips as the ride down is begun.

Another error is allowing the hips to drop back, as in a sitting position. This motion will cause a force outward which will be increased by the press into the dive. It is safe to say that the trajectory of a dive will follow a line through two points: the ball of the foot and the hip joint. If the hips are set back 45 degrees from the end of the board, the dive will travel in low arc from the board. To correct this error, keep the shoulders directly over the hips, the hips directly over the heels, and the whole body weight resting over the balls of the feet throughout the entire action.

The third common error is starting the actions used to perform the dive before leaving the board. This is a usual mistake of one who is learning a back dive. On the first attempt you may be apprehensive, and uncertain about the outcome of your effort. It is natural enough that you should worry about landing flat on the dive, and you may try to prevent this by throwing your arms and head backward with too great a thrust, thus rotating your body too much and passing the vertical point of entry.

The three errors just described will cause a poor dive—but they are not dangerous. The most serious error is the one commonly called the "crow hop," which means bouncing the board rather than riding it. This error is dangerous because it often causes the feet to shift, either forward or backward, and as a result the diver may slip off the board during the press, striking his shins or some part of his body on the board. Sometimes your feet may move from their original position and you will not even be aware of it. In this case, the error may be difficult to correct. The real cause of the error is lifting the arms and heels too vigorously in starting the motion of the board in preparation for the dive.

If you have this fault, it may be that the diving board flexibility does not suit your natural rhythm for taking off in a back dive, and the error can be eliminated by adjusting the fulcrum. However, it is always necessary to think clearly during the start of your back dive and to remember not to lift your arms too high or too fast, or with too great a force. This also applies to the heel lift. A smooth arm lift and heel lift, in perfect rhythm with the board, will completely eliminate all danger of slipping off the board.

8. Back Dive (Pike)

The trend toward the use of the back header in the pike position may have had its beginnings in the preparations for the 1952 Olympic Games. At that time the degree of difficulty of this dive was higher than that of the back dive in layout position, and the American divers realized that it worked into a list of required dives that would total the 11.0 degrees of difficulty which was the maximum allowed in the first five dives. Also the mechanics of the back dive in the pike position make it much easier to control than in the layout position, and adjustments can be made while the dive is actually being performed.

Briefly, the Back Dive Pike can be described as a perfectly straight upward thrust from the board, with an immediate leg lift made by a deep hip flexion. The position at the top of the lift is an inverted jackknife. Once in this position you have only to drop backward with the trunk and place your arms over your head to achieve a true vertical entry. The adjustments that can be made in doing this dive in pike position are many. For example, if your legs are not coming up into position fast enough to give the proper amount of rotation at the peak of the dive, it is easy to hold the pike until the legs reach the proper angle, and then open. If they come up too fast, you have a chance to let them drop back as you fall back with your upper body. These are only two possible adjustments. There are others which can be made with the arm movement as the opening is made.

In the execution of this dive you should be sure that your lift is perpendicular to the end of the board. When you press from the board be sure to lift your arms up above your head but forward of your face. As soon as your feet have left the board, start to raise your legs to form a pike position. When your legs are nearly perpendicular to the water, bring your hands forward to touch your toes. To keep your legs in this perfect position as your trunk drops backward to open the pike you must bring your arms side-outward in a lateral plane with

your upper body as they swing overhead for your entry. If you swing
your arms in front of your body, your legs may drop backward and
cause a lower back arch. This type of movement of the legs and back
causes the entry to be either short or long, depending upon the force
of the arm swing.

9. Back Dive (Layout)

The back header in layout position is one of the most beautiful
and graceful of all dives. Unfortunately it is seldom seen today because the dive in the pike position, which now has the same degree
of difficulty rating, is more easily controlled. However, the layout
dive should be one of every diver's skills because it stimulates poise
and grace, as well as precision in movements.

In all backward takeoff dives, balance while working the board
is very important. To get the proper direction from the board you
must keep your weight on the end of the board as you press up perpendicular to it. Swing your arms forward-upward and begin to
spread them above your head as you leave the board, at the same time
lifting your chest. The combination of arm and chest lift will start
you upward and supply the necessary rotating force. Tilting the head
back is also an aid which should be coordinated into the whole action,
but avoid snapping the head backward with force. The proper lift
of the head can probably be described most clearly in terms of the
amount of movement that the chin makes upward: roughly three
inches.

One of the most important parts of this dive is the control of your
pelvic region. It is absolutely necessary that you set this middle part
of your body to insure the proper leg lift. Without a firm abdomen
and lower back you will hinge at the waist, and the legs will not
follow the arc established by the arm, chest, and head lift. As you
turn over at the top of the lift, your arms should be spread to a line

straight through the shoulders, and they are held in this position until just before the entry. As you pass through this turning-over phase of the dive, look for the water and pick the spot where you plan to enter. When you are headed downward and nearly vertical, bring your arms together overhead with your hands together. In this position you will open a hole in the surface of the water for a clean entry. To flatten your back and remove the arch, bring the head back to a normal position in line with the body.

Through the complete dive keep your knees straight and your feet in full extension with the toes pointed.

IV: REVERSE DIVES

The reverse dive in either the pike or the layout position should be learned shortly after you have developed your back dives. In execution the reverse dives discussed in this part are much like the back dives described previously.

10. Reverse Dive (Layout)

The Reverse Dive in layout position can be compared to the Back Dive Layout in appearance and in method of execution. The graceful arc through which both these dives pass is probably the most beautiful in all springboard diving.

To execute this dive, you must know that the rotating force is created by the movements of the arms, head, and chest, and that the legs must follow the arc thus established. In order to insure this action, the midsection of the body must be held firm and not allowed to sag.

The dive is started with a forward approach which must be in good balance. The hurdle should be reasonably high and drop you perpendicular to the end of the board. As you ride the board through its bending action, you must remain perpendicular to the board. Any bending from the waist will thrust you out from the board, and leaning forward will prevent the dive from rotating in the easy manner necessary to portray a graceful movement. As you leave the board, your arms must be above your head, spreading to a position straight through the shoulders. This arm movement is combined with a chest and head lift at the same time to start the whole body rotating backward toward the water. To make the lower body follow in the arc established by the arms, head, and chest, contract the muscles of the abdomen and buttocks. As you turn over at the top of the lift and start downward, head first, look for the water, and when it is visible bring your arms together overhead for the entry. Also, the head should be brought forward to remove the arch from the back and give a good alignment to the dive upon entry.

11. Reverse Dive (Pike)

The directions for the Back Dive Pike can be used for this dive also. The only difference is a result of the manner in which you use the springboard. Since the reverse is performed from a forward approach, the thrust from the board will be stronger than in a back dive. With this more forceful thrust, the lift will be higher and the rotation faster, so some adjustments to lessen rotation must be made.

For the proper rotation you will need to stretch your arms above your head but not allow them to move backward past a vertical line. The arms are then moved forward to meet the legs as they near the perpendicular to the water. This arm action will stop any excessive rotation and will give you the same control in this dive as you have in the back header in the pike position.

V: INWARD DIVES

The Inward Dive is the first in its group (see page 4) and, therefore, one of the five required dives. The pike position of this dive, which has a degree of difficulty rating of 1.3, is often referred to as the Back Jackknife. Recently the layout position has become popular from the one-meter board because of the higher degree of difficulty (1.7) awarded it since 1957.

12. Inward Dive (Pike)

One of the most important factors in doing the Inward Dive in the pike position is balance during the backward takeoff. If your arm action is in keeping with the techniques set forth on pages 23-25, you will be in the best position for a good inward pike as you are thrust from the board. Remember: during the board work your arms should be raised laterally and only reach a point slightly above your head as you rise onto your toes. From this position the arms are brought down, slightly forward, with great force as the knees flex in preparation for bending the board downward. Then your arms are swung upward, passing in front of your face with a slight bend at the elbows. Combined with the leg thrust, this arm action forces your whole body up from the board. During the entire board work you should feel that all your weight is supported over the balls of the feet.

After your arms reach above your head for the lift there should be a bending at the hips even before your feet have left the board. This bending, although slight, is important to the execution of the dive because it allows you to push the hips upward early enough to complete the pike at the highest point in the lift.

During the flight upward the legs should be held perpendicular to the water. This will eliminate excessive rotation as the trunk is bent forward and the hands are placed on the top of the insteps to form a deep pike position. When the trunk has rotated to the vertical, allow the legs to swing backward and line up with the trunk. As usual on all head-first entries, place your arms alongside the head, straight at the elbows, with your hands together. Throughout the entire dive you should see the water for better control of the entry.

VI: TWIST DIVES

The Forward Dive One-half Twist is by far the most difficult of the basic dives. It is known as "the great separator" in most championship competitions because so many execute it poorly and only outstanding divers do it well. Simple errors which are often concealed in other dives, becoming scarcely evident in the end result, are magnified in a one-half twist to glaring mistakes. For example, a lateral cast on leaving the board may not be apparent in many dives because all motions are in the same direction. But the same amount of lateral cast from the board in a one-half twist will be increased by the mechanics of the dive so that the cast is obvious at the entry. A twist dive which is cut off from the board before the press is complete will be disastrous because the legs will rise too fast, whereas early action into most other dives may go unnoticed. Since this dive is quite sensitive to error, be very particular with your fundamentals.

13. Forward Dive One-half Twist (Layout)

Before you begin this dive it is important to master a good forward layout position, for all the essentials of a Forward Dive Layout or "Swan" Dive are here, with the addition of a one-half twist. There are many ways of describing the mechanics of the twist. It has been said, for example, that the diver starts as for a swan dive and drops one shoulder toward the water to initiate the twist. Another description is that the diver drops one arm and looks down it toward the water, causing a slight spiral turn of the body.

My experience in teaching this dive indicates that most of the common errors can be eliminated if the diver visualizes a front dive layout with a one-quarter turn until the legs have risen to a position above the head, followed by an additional one-quarter turn as he descends toward the water, head first. In performing the dive in this manner there is no doubt that, since the body is going to twist a quarter-turn early in the dive, some of the twisting must be started from the board. This twisting force should be very slight and smooth so that the dive appears to be the same as a swan dive.

The takeoff from the board is the same as for a front dive layout except that a twist is started by moving the arms to left or right. (For the purpose of establishing reference to direction of twists, a turn which spirals the front of the body toward the diver's left is called a left twist, and a turn the opposite way is called a right twist.) It is amazing how, merely by desiring to execute a twist, a diver will unconsciously move in a manner that will produce some spiral rotation. However, these movements may be fundamentally wrong and lead to faulty habits which are difficult to correct.

The movements initiating the twist are begun as you swing your arms overhead on leaving the board. To perform the one-half twist with a left twist, swing your right arm up as for a swan dive but point it directly to the far end of the pool. At the same time swing your left arm into a swan position above your head but pull it backward, causing your whole body to twist to the left as you leave the board.

To give you the feel of the arm action just described, and an understanding of what it will do, practice the movements in front of a large mirror. Stand directly in front of the mirror so that you have a full view of your body. Swing the right arm through as described above, pointing it directly at the mirror; at the same time swing the left arm toward the mirror and then pull back with the shoulder. You will see the upper body start to twist. After repeating this exercise several times before the mirror, add another movement to help you get the feel of this dive. Lift the left leg back and free of the floor, with the knee straight, the ankle extended, and the toes pointed as the arm action is made. As mentioned before, the arm action is the determining factor in making the body twist in this dive. Therefore, avoid any unnecessary twisting of your head.

Now try putting these fundamentals to work for a complete dive twisting to the left. During the approach remain straight through the hips, and as the board lifts your body upward, swing your arms into the practiced position, which will produce the first one-quarter twist. Raise both legs up behind in the manner of the single leg lift you practiced in front of the mirror. As the legs rise the whole body will rotate and begin to head downward. The right arm will be pointing directly at the water, and you will see the water beyond your right hand. Now you should move your left arm around to meet your right arm over your head. Be sure to keep the left arm well behind your head to continue the twisting movement. When your arms come together for a vertical entry the added one-quarter twist will have been made and you will enter the water in a position similar to that in a back dive. However, the entry will feel like that of a front dive.

VII: SOMERSAULTS

This discussion of spin techniques is important to your performance of optional dives in competition, for excepting the "basic dives" in each of the five groups, nearly every dive listed in the official table (see page 4) is a somersault of one form or another. Since the spin is either forward or backward in all spinning dives, mastering the fundamentals of the forward and back somersault dives prepares you for learning inward and reverse somersaults, respectively, as well as the more complicated spinning twists.

In attempting the spinning dives you will discover that when the body leaves the board in a near-perpendicular it can be thrown higher and with more force because the full thrust of the springboard is behind the upward movement. You will begin to understand the value of an upright position on the takeoff, for extra speed and elevation are especially necessary in dives with multiple movements. But the idea that maximum lift must be reached before the tuck or pike is begun is completely wrong. You should begin the actions for gathering into the spin position as soon as you are in the air; these movements do not diminish lift if they are not begun until after the diver's feet leave the board.

A tuck is the fastest and easiest position in which to execute a spin dive. The keys to fast spinning are a tight tuck or pike and a proper manner of executing the movement. To learn how a good tuck position should look and feel, sit on the deck of the pool and flex the knees and hips, bringing the thighs tight against the chest. Place the hands on the legs about halfway between the ankles and knees, palms resting on the sides of the legs, and fingers on the shins. The arms should pull in hard to give the necessary tightness to the tuck, the elbows should be close to the sides, and the toes pointed.

Although the pike position is considered to be a more difficult way of rotating for dives of more than one and one-half spins, it is by far the more popular position, where a choice is possible, because it is more attractive and graceful and easier ·to control. In dives which combine multiple twists with multiple somersaults the pike position must be used. The diver performing a full twisting one-and-one-half somersault, for example, must spin in the pike position in order to straighten out for the twists and return to spinning position to continue the rotation.

It is important to know that a spin in tuck position cannot be *stopped* by a kickout to straight position, but it can be *slowed down* by the kickout so that you can enter the water vertically. Because the speed of the spin and the method used to slow it vary with the diver, it is impossible to state exactly when the opening should be made. Only through practice will you be able to discover the right moment.

14. Forward Spinning

To understand the fundamentals of forward spinning, which apply to all forward and inward somersault dives, you must realize that the hip lift contributes more to body rotation than does any other movement. The downward thrust of the arms, head, and upper body plays an important part, but this movement must follow the action of the hips.

Probably the first optional dive that you will want to attempt is the Forward One-and-one-half Somersault. This dive is far easier to perform and requires less experience than the Forward Somersault; yet there is often a greater feeling of accomplishment in learning it because of the extra one-half spin. Spinning forward one and one-half times is almost a natural movement from the one-meter board, whereas one somersault requires exact timing in execution. Another reason the one-and-one-half is considered easier is that your head is down as you complete the spins and you are able to see the water for the entry. You can dismiss any fears you may have about attempting a dive of this sort. The worst thing that can happen to you in such a dive from the one-meter board is a flat landing, and this does little more than sting your skin; it can do no serious harm. The discomfort of a sting lasts only a minute or two.

For the Forward One-and-one-half Somersault (tuck), begin with a good forward approach and a controlled drop to the end of the board. After the board has been pressed down and begins to rise you should swing your arms above your head, allowing them to bend slightly at the elbows as they pass your face. You should be perpendicular to the board as you complete the press. This position will enable you to get the greatest amount of lift in your initial hip movement, and your rotation will be fast and at a high elevation, increasing the time for completing all the movements of the dive before you reach the water. There should be a slight forward bending at the waist while you are still on the board. Naturally, you must not bend so far forward that the dive will be performed too low and too far out, but in order to spin forcefully, you should be in a position that lends itself to the movement desired. All other actions used to gather in the tuck are delayed until the hips have been given a full thrust upward.

As soon as you feel the hips being raised, begin to bend your knees and bring the heels in toward the buttocks. The arms, head, and upper body are then thrust downward to complete the tuck, the hands grasping the front of the legs and the arms pulling the chest in tight to the thighs. Your chin should be above your knees so that you will get a clear view of the water as you spin forward. This position is held until you have rotated beyond one and one-quarter turns; then the tuck is opened.

To open from the tuck position, push your legs away from your chest to a straight line through the hips and knees, and at the same time lift your chest and place your arms over your head so that your body will enter the water in a true vertical line. A forward spin dive should enter the water not less than three feet and not more than seven feet from the diving end of the board.

Two common errors which you should take care to avoid in executing forward somersault dives are: (1) leaning too far forward from the board while riding out the press, and (2) bringing the arms, head, and shoulders downward into spin position before the hips have sufficient lift. Such actions will result in a head-chasing-feet effect, and the result is an open tuck at low elevation. This type of spin is usually uncontrolled, and difficult to stop for a clean entry. A dive performed with the first error will be too far out from the end of the board, while the second error very often brings the dive too close to the board.

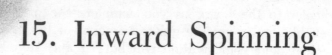

15. Inward Spinning

The spin techniques for inward somersault dives are the same as for forward spinning dives, but the takeoff is backward. The Inward Somersault and Inward One-and-one-half Somersault in tuck position begin like the Inward Dive (pike) described on pages 31-32. Of course, the power applied to the arm throw and hip lift must be greater for the somersaults than for the simple header.

Arm action and hip position during the board work are key factors in getting this dive started in the proper direction. When the arms are raised they should be allowed to bend as they pass in front of the body to a position just above the head. They should reach this position about the time that your hips are being thrust upward. Control of the hips is discussed in more detail in the description of the backward takeoff (pages 23-25). Basically, the control is established by proper arm swing during the board work and by keeping the hips directly over the balls of the feet. Do not swing the arms down behind your back or set the hips back over the water as you prepare to leave the board. Only by a complete awareness of the position of your hips can you be sure that you will leave the board in the proper direction. As in all inward dives, perfect balance while working the board for the takeoff is particularly essential. Any backward leaning of the upper body will work against a good forward rotation.

The one basic difference between the start of the inward header and the inward somersault dives is the action of the legs as you leave the board. You will recall that in the inward header (pike) the spin must be retarded by holding the legs perpendicular to the water as the trunk is laid down to close the pike. In the somersault dives this movement is not used; instead, an action which *produces* rotation is made. To increase the speed of the spin when doing an inward somersault in tuck position, you allow the legs to swing backward as you bend the knees and bring the heels up toward the buttocks. After the hips have risen, force the arms, head, and trunk down and gather into a tight tuck position.

It is quite possible that as you stand in position to attempt this dive for the first time you will wonder how you can avoid hitting the board when you spin forward from your backward stance. Actually this dive is no more dangerous than the inward header if you take care to complete the press before starting the spin. Often the beginner will either jump backward before starting the spin or will cut his lift by moving into the spin too early. Jumping backward will cause a slow spin, which will lessen the chances of your performing a complete somersault before hitting the water. But starting the spin before the press is complete can be really dangerous, for the dive will be too close to the board. By using the same takeoff for this dive as is used for the inward header you will be in no danger of hitting the board—and the execution of the somersault will be easy.

The single somersault should be attempted before the one-and-one-half if you are working from the one-meter board. From the three-meter level, however, it is advisable to do the one-and-one-half first because it is easier—and from the higher board you will have plenty of time to perform it.

For the single somersault in tuck position it is especially important to open the tuck at the proper point in the rotation. While you are learning, your coach or a friend can assist you by calling you out of the tuck at the proper time. It is important not to open too early on this dive because your feet may be pushed in over the board, rather than toward the water, if the body is extended too soon. The somersault should be nearly completed before you straighten out of the tuck. Even with a good high spin at a safe distance from the board, kicking out at three-quarters of a turn could allow the feet to strike the board. Hitting the board with the feet is not dangerous, but it does often frighten a beginning diver. For this reason it is better to open late in early attempts at this dive.

The tuck is opened by pushing the legs away from the chest to a straight line through the hips and knees, at the same time lifting the chest so that the body will be in an erect standing position as the feet enter the water. The arms should be straight down at your sides, with the hands on the outside of the thighs.

The one-and-one-half somersault in tuck position is made in the same manner as the single somersault, but the speed is increased by applying more force to the hip lift and arm thrust as you begin the tuck, and the tuck is held longer. When you have turned over beyond one and one-quarter turns, push the legs outward from the tuck position into a straight line with the trunk, and bring the arms overhead. In this dive you will be able to see the water as you open the tuck and make your entry in a true vertical line.

After you have mastered the inward somersault from the one-meter board in tuck position, try the one-and-one-half somersault from the three-meter board in pike position.

16. Backward Spinning

Because the spin is backward in backward and reverse somersault dives, the mechanics of spinning are the same for both groups. For backward dives you leave the board with your back to the water; for reverse dives you start with a forward approach to the end of the board and then rotate backward over the water as you perform the spins.

To spin backward in tuck position the rotation is begun during the thrust from the board by raising the arms, chest, and head. As the arms swing upward above the head, the chest is given a lift in the same direction and the head a slight tilt backward. These movements are immediately followed by a lifting of the legs into tuck position. Then the arms are dropped down to grasp the shins and pulled in hard to tighten the thighs to the chest. As always when the tuck position is used, the tightness of the tuck is of great importance because it largely determines the speed of rotation.

Your first attempt at a backward spin should be the Back Somersault (tuck), but before trying it reread the section on the backward takeoff (pages 23-25). There are two important fundamentals that must be remembered in performing a backward spin from a backward takeoff: (1) the arms must not reach back behind the head, and (2) the hips must remain directly over the balls of the feet while you are working the board. Although the natural tendency in preparing for a backward spin is to reach backward with arms, head, and chest with great force, this is far from the proper form. True, a spin can be produced by this method, but it will be uncontrolled, and you will have difficulty in stopping the rotation. Also, this manner of spinning will lower the elevation of the spin, greatly diminishing the chances for a good dive; the spin will usually be too far out from the end of the board.

In this dive you will enter the water feet first, with the body in full extension. When three-quarters of a full turn has been made in the tuck, the spin is opened by thrusting the legs away from the chest and straightening the hips and knees. At the same time the chest will lift as the back straightens and the arms are placed at the sides. The last one-quarter somersault will be made by the carry-over force •from the tuck position. On entry, your body should be in a vertical line, with your arms straight at your sides.

After you have performed a back somersault with success the next challenge will be the Back One-and-one-half Somersault (tuck). Fundamentally, all actions for this dive are the same as for the single somersault, although entry into the water is made head first. Of course, because of the extra half spin, more force must be applied to all movements, and the time spent in the tuck position will seem much longer. You will actually be in the tuck more than twice as long as for the single somersault, because opening for the single comes shortly after the complete gather in, whereas the opening for this new dive will not start until one and one-quarter turns have been made.

The tuck should be opened by kicking out strongly, extending the legs from the hips and straightening the knees. After this movement, give the head a backward thrust so that you will see the water before entering it. When the head is well back, the arms should be brought overhead in line with the upper body. Because this dive spins at a terrific speed, it is necessary to kick out strongly in this manner and to delay the action of the arms to retard the spin and give better control on entry. If the arms are swung overhead at the same time that the legs are extended, the force that the legs exert against the direction of the spin will be neutralized, and the dive will cast long on entry. However, if you kick out of the tuck too early, it is advantageous to bring the arms overhead at the same time that the head is thrown backward, in order to continue the rotation to the proper angle of entry.

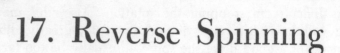

17. Reverse Spinning

Mastery of the back somersault dives will equip you for learning the reverse somersault, for the mechanics of the spin are the same in both types of dive. The differences are a result of the different direction of takeoff—backward for back spins, forward for reverse.

Your first endeavor should be a reverse somersault in tuck position. No doubt some apprehension will accompany your first attempt at this dive, but there is only one possible mistake that would place you in danger of physical harm. That is the failure to take a complete ride and press from the board before moving into the spin. If the takeoff is hurried, and the head, arms, and chest are thrown backward too soon, the diver will fall into a slipping motion and may strike the board with his head. This uncontrolled spin is the result of a low point of rotation. To bring out vividly the nature of this motion, it might be compared to the movement of a person who slips on a patch of ice. His feet swing out from under him, his body rotates upward in reverse, and he lands on his back at the spot from which his feet slipped. Simply by being certain to take a complete ride and press you will eliminate all danger of this type of accident in a reverse spinning dive.

In performing a full reverse, your approach to the end of the board must be standard and in good balance. Upon leaving the board, raise the arms upward in front to a point above the head, and tilt the head back slightly. These two moves will lift the chest and start the backward rotation. Add to this early turning the leg lift into tuck position immediately upon leaving the board, for bringing the legs up will make the body turn with greater speed. Drop the arms down to grasp the shins and pull in hard to tighten the thighs to the chest. The release from the tuck must be made when the rotation is about three-quarters complete. All opening movements are the same as those used in the backward somersault.

After you have become proficient in the single somersault from the one-meter board you will want to try the reverse one-and-one-half. Except for the board work the only difference between the reverse and the back one-and-one-half is the timing. The tuck position must necessarily be held longer for reverse somersaults because the momentum from the forward approach will decrease the speed of backward rotation. (Also, on your first attempt you will probably lean forward somewhat from the board, increasing the momentum contrary to reverse spinning and thus making the dive more difficult to perform.) But it is also true that the elevation gained from a full forward approach will be higher than that from a standing backward takeoff, and this extra lift will give you more time to perform the dive. The execution of the spin and kickout are the same in both dives.

Many divers avoid this dive because they fear hitting the board. As noted above, the only error which can cause you any danger is leaving the board too soon, and all danger can be eliminated if a controlled, balanced hurdle and a complete press are made.

18. Forward One-and-one-half with One Twist

"Full twister" is the abbreviated term for the one-and-one-half somersault with one twist. This dive was developed by the United States divers in the late 1920s and performed by such outstanding men as Pete Desjardins, Micky Riley, and Dutch Smith. The manner of executing the dive at that time did not resemble the style of today in any way. As performed by these champions, the dive was not opened from a deep pike position during the twist. This method could be used successfully for a single twist, but it would never permit the diver to add more than one twist while doing a one-and-one-half somersault.

The method used today is to open the pike as the twist is applied so that the body is in full extension, making possible a spiral twist. This modern method allows the diver to complete two twists with the one-and-one-half somersault. The double twister was listed as a dive for competition in the United States in 1947, and for competition in the Olympic Games in 1948. Since many divers today are able to twist three times with complete control, it is more than likely that the triple twister will soon be added to the official list of dives.

Before learning this dive you must master the simple forward somersault in pike position from the one-meter board. When you are able to do it and know exactly where you are in the turn at all times, begin to straighten out from the pike after rotating one-half somersault. Naturally the force applied to this semi-open somersault must be greater than for the completely piked turn. When you are able to perform the somersault with this opening and enter the water feet first you will be ready to begin applying the twist.

Twisting in the straight body position can be learned by standing on the deck of the pool and practicing the arm movements which produce the twist. Before you begin you must determine in which direction you twist more naturally; it will not necessarily be the same direction for this dive as for your forward dive with one-half twist. To start a twist both arms must be moved at the same time in the direction that you want to turn. To twist to your left, for example, bring your left arm up and behind your head as your right arm swings across your chest. Your left elbow may bend slightly but be sure to keep the upper arm in close to the back of your head. As you practice these arm movements in a standing position you will feel a distant twist of the upper body and realize the ease with which a twist can be made.

Your first attempt to twist while somersaulting will leave you completely confused and lost—and quite surprised when you land in the water feet first. You will probably not know whether or not you made a twist. But after repeating this part of the dive many times you will begin to see the water before you enter it, and then your control of the whole dive will steadily improve.

Since twisting in this straight position is so easy, it will be necessary for you to learn a method for stopping at the completion of the full twist. To do this you must combine two actions. The first move is to bring your arms down to a position used in the forward one-

and-one-half somersault open pike, that is, they should be in a straight line through the shoulders, at right angles to your sides. The other action which eliminates the twisting force is a return to the pike position by bending at the hips. However, if you wish to do only a single somersault the bend should be made by bringing the legs up into a pike rather than bending forward with the trunk.

The complete dive, the one-and-one-half somersault with one twist, can be accomplished when you are able to do the preliminary phase (just described) from the one-meter board. All that remains is the addition of the last one-half somersault, which allows you to enter the water head first. This is made possible by a greater rotating force from the board. The needed increase in the speed of the spin is made by giving the hips a stronger thrust and by applying more downward drive into the pike position with your arms, head, and upper body. When the twist is completed and the arms are extended outward in a line with the shoulder to stop the twist, immediately bend at the waist, returning the body to a deep pike position to continue the spin. The whole dive can be accomplished more easily from the three-meter board because of the additional space available.

Your success in performing this dive is dependent upon your opening from the pike position to a straight position while twisting. When the forward rotation is followed by a strong kickout to a straight line the twist can be applied as soon as the opening begins. Another important factor is that you must be perfectly square with your shoulders when leaving the board. If the twist is anticipated, and begun while the feet are still in contact with the board, the dive will have a lateral cast which will be evident in the entry because it will usually result in an inability to stop the twist at the proper time.

VIII: SAVES

Usually, if a diver is approaching the water at the wrong angle for a vertical entry he will realize his error and can adjust his entry before it is spoiled. The technique which will thus correct a dive faulty on entry is called a "save," an underwater gymnastic which brings the feet to the vertical before they strike the water and raise a splash. The reverse save, which we will consider first, has been used by divers since the mid-1930s. The forward somersault save is a newer technique, dating back to the early 1950s.

The Reverse Save As Seen from Above the Water.
(The diving board is to the left. The reverse save shown is being used in a reverse one-and-one-half or a one-half reverse.)

The Forward Save As Seen from Above the Water.
(The diving board is to the left. The forward save shown is used in any multiple spin forward dive.)

19. Reverse Save

A reverse save is used to correct a backward spinning dive, such as the one-and-one-half back or the one-and-one-half reverse, which has been opened too late for a vertical entry. Basically, the technique is to continue the established arc of the body as it descends into the water, arching the back and bending the knees to bring the lower legs to the vertical before they can cast a splash long. The lower back, head, and arms must be used in executing an effective reverse save.

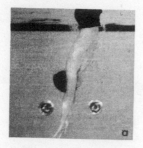

The Reverse Save

In the photographs above, the diver is first shown (*a*) beyond a vertical line in his entry after submerging past his waist. (The dark horizontal line indicates the level of the water.) As he descends further (*b*) he begins to arch his back, an action which will help bring the lower legs, still above the surface, back into a vertical line. The arch becomes greater (*c*) as he begins to elevate his head. Bending the knees (*d*) keeps the feet vertical and pulls them quickly beneath the surface to minimize the splash. The diver also uses his arms (*e*) to make the entry shallow. With his legs deeply bent, (*f*) he scoops his arms to pull his head and chest toward the surface.

20. Forward Save

Skippy Browning, the 1952 Olympic Champion, used the forward somersault save to control his entries on all forward dives. His soft entry into the water and vertical drop beneath it gave him the margin of victory over his contemporaries, and his methods were carefully

The Forward Save

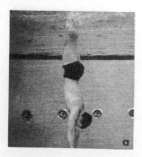
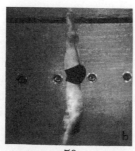
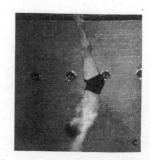

The Reverse Save

studied by all divers of that time. Although the technique was copied with a fair degree of success, the first tendency was to use the save when it was not necessary. On many occasions dives which were perfectly good were ruined in the entry by unwise use of the save. Today, however, refinement in the usage of the forward save has given divers another means toward perfection in performance.

In order to clearly illustrate the results of the forward save technique, the diver's movements are shown (below) completely below the surface of the water. He has actually made a perfect entry, (*a*) and is descending straight toward the bottom of the pool. (In using the forward save to correct a faulty angle of entry you will begin the movements shown above while your lower legs are still above the surface.) The diver begins to correct (*b*) by bringing his head and arms forward to initiate a forward somersault (pike). The result of the pike can be seen (*c*) in the new angle of the legs with the horizontal line. (When the legs are past the vertical at the beginning of the entry, this movement brings them back perpendicular to the water surface for a splashless entry.) As the pike deepens, the diver spreads his arms to the sides (*d*), and pulls (*e*) to help the piking action and (*f*) turn his upper body toward the surface. This deep pike position is completely under the water and has no effect on the dive at this point.

The Forward Save

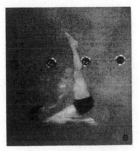

GLOSSARY OF DIVING TERMS

Approach: The three-step run and hurdle used in performing a dive in which the diver faces the water for the takeoff.

Back dive: A header which rotates backward from a backward takeoff.

Backward takeoff: The combination of movements performed on the end of the board with the back to the water in preparation for a back or inward dive.

Cast, lateral: A slight twist of a dive to left or right which originates in the take-off from the board as a result of poor balance.

Cast long: To pass the proper point for vertical entry so that the dive enters the water at an angle. Unless a *Save* is used, the legs do not enter the water cleanly but fall over, raising a splash.

Cast short: To fall short of the proper point of entry.

Cutaway dive: A common name for an inward dive, usually one in which one or more somersaults are completed.

Degree of difficulty: The rating, or value, of each dive, based on difficulty of performance. The degrees of difficulty range by tenths from 1.2 for the simplest dives (e.g., forward dive in tuck position from the one-meter board) to 2.8 for the dive rated most difficult (reverse two-and-one-half somersault in tuck position from the three-meter board). See pages 4 and 5 for table listing degree of difficulty for all dives.

Drop: The descent from the highest point in the hurdle to the end of the board.

Entry: The final part of the dive, beginning when the diver's hands touch the water.

Forward dive: A dive which rotates forward from a forward approach. Sometimes referred to also as a front dive.

Full Twister: A term often used for the forward one-and-one-half somersault with one twist.

Gainer: Another name for a reverse somersault.

Gather in: Movement into the *Tuck* position.

Half Gainer: Another name for the reverse header.

Header: A dive which rotates the body one-half turn before it enters the water.

Hurdle: The jump to the end of the board following the three-step run in the forward approach.

Inward dive: A dive which rotates forward from a backward takeoff.

Jackknife: Another name for an inward or forward header in pike position.

Layout: One of the three positions in which dives may be performed. In the layout the body is held straight through the hips and knees and the arms are spread to the sides.

Lift: The elevation of the body as it rises from the board in the performance of a dive.

Opening: Straightening the body from a tuck or pike position.

Overthrow: The falling over of the legs as the result of a nonvertical entry.

Pike: One of the three positions in which a dive may be performed. In the pike the body is deeply bent at the hips with the legs held straight through the knees, and the arms straight at the elbows.

Press: The act of straightening the legs and raising the arms to leave the spring-board.

Reverse dive: A dive which rotates backward from a forward takeoff.

Ride down: The part of the dive, following the drop from the hurdle, in which the knees are bent and the arms swung down to prepare for the *Press.*

Rotate: An action in which the diver turns heels over head from the board.

Run: The three steps taken before the hurdle in a forward approach to a dive. These steps are now usually taken at a walking gait.

Save: An underwater gymnastic used by the diver to prevent an overthrow of his legs after a non-vertical entry. The two types are the reverse and forward.

Somersault dive: A dive which spins.

Spin: The action of rotating one or more full turns.

Swan: Another name for a forward dive performed in layout position.

Takeoff: The lift of the body from the end of the board into the dive.

Thrust: The force with which the body is pushed upward from the springboard after a *Press.*

Tuck: One of the three positions in which dives may be performed. In the tuck the body is bunched, with the hips flexed, the knees bent, and the thighs held tight against the trunk by the hands, which grasp the shins.

Twist dive: A dive in which the body spirals laterally. In the full twist the body spirals through 360 degrees; in the half twist, through 180 degrees. The twisting dives form the largest of the five basic groups of dives since a twist may be added to any dive in any direction.

Walk: A term used for the three steps in the forward approach technically known as the *Run.*

FLIP
SEQUENCE
SERIES

The dives shown in the following flip sequence series are perhaps the most essential in the development of the diver. They encompass all of the movements necessary in the performance of any dive listed in the Swimming Guides of the National Amateur Athletic Union and the National Collegiate Athletic Association. Besides the forward approach, there are five series showing a basic dive in each of the five groups: Forward, Backward, Reverse, Inward, and Twisting. In any contest—from the Olympic Games to your local meet—these dives must be performed. But remember that these dives are "basic" only in the *direction* of the dive. They are very far from including every movement that you, as a diver, will need to make. Therefore, the other six dives of the flip sequence have been carefully chosen so that you will be able to see clearly *every* action ever performed by a diver. With these dives at your command you can enter any contest—you might even become a champion—and you will certainly add greatly to your legitimate pride and pleasure in a good performance.

The pictures are studies of the 1956 Olympic Diving Champion, Bob Clotworthy. The dives were performed from the one-meter springboard at the Payne Whitney Gymnasium of Yale University.

The flip sequence series is easy to use. In each of the twelve series there are twenty pictures, arranged consecutively. Series Numbers 1, 2, 3, 7, 8, and 9 are on odd-numbered, right-hand pages; Series 4, 5, 6, 10, 11, and 12 are on even-numbered, left-hand pages. To study Flip Sequence Series No. 1 (Forward Approach), for example, hold the book in your left hand and flip through pages 57-97 with your right thumb. For Series 4 (Back Dive Layout) just reverse the process: hold the book in your right hand and, starting at page 98, flip backward in the book with your left thumb.

You will notice that each picture carries a brief commentary which relates it to the whole dive and points out especially important movements. By looking at each picture separately you can study the segments of the dive. This will be of particular help to you in finding out where you may be going wrong and how to correct your error.

Whether flipped at speed or studied individually, these pictures will bring you into association with one of the great champions and will constantly aid you in your understanding, practice, and accomplishment in the sport of diving.

[*You may wish to cut out the strip indicated by the double lines between photos for easier flipping of the pages and a better total picture of each sequence.*]

1. Forward Approach

2. Forward Dive (Pike)

3. Back Dive (Pike)

1. Forward Approach

1—1. The diver takes his first step of a three-step and hurdle approach. (In this series of pictures the diver will start his approach with his right leg and use the same leg for his hurdle press.)

2. Forward Dive (Pike)

1—2. The diver passes over the highest point in his hurdle.

3. Back Dive (Pike)

1—3. The diver stands motionless after dropping arms to sides. Note that he is using the four-movement technique described on page 24. (Careful observation of photos 1–3 through 8–3 will show that the diver is looking straight forward. It is advisable to focus either on the fixed end of the board or at a spot at eye level. You will have less difficulty adjusting to outdoor diving if you establish your focal point at the fixed end of the board.)

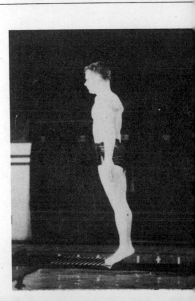

20—4. The diver is completely submerged, but continues to stretch to the bottom.

20—5. The diver pulls in the lower legs quickly by using a reverse save, eliminating any possibility of overthrow of the feet.

20—6. Only the smallest splash is seen due to the perfect alignment and entry in this dive.

2–1. The diver is halfway between his first and second step. (Notice the casual swing of the arms in these early steps.)

2–2. He has brought his legs together as he descends toward the board. His arms are also dropping side-downward.

2–3. The heels have dropped to set the board in motion, and the arms begin to lift-side-upward.

19—4. This photo shows absolute perfection in foot position to the very end of the dive. Quite often this very important part of the dive is neglected.

19—5. The lower legs are straight up as the diver works his back and bends his knees under water to effect an entry which appears to be vertical.

19—6. As the lower legs and feet begin to submerge, the whole body continues straight toward the bottom. (Notice the perfect point of the feet and toes.)

3—1. He places the left foot on the board for end of second step. (Notice it is a heel–toe contact with the board.)

3—2. Just before striking the board, he bends his knees slightly and flattens his feet so that he will land on the balls of his feet.

3—3. Arms continue to rise, as the diver pushes up onto his toes.

18—4. The shadow beneath the water indicates how the diver descends straight downward to the bottom of the pool.

18—5. The diver's legs follow through the hole opened by the arms and upper body.

18—6. Perfect position is shown in this picture prior to entering the water. (Notice the head is between the arms and the body is pointing arrowlike toward the water.)

4—1. The weight is directly over the foot as the heel comes in firm contact with the board.

4—2. As contact is made with the board, his knees continue to bend deeper, and his arms are nearly at the bottom of their downswing.

4—3. Arms and heels continue action upward.

17—4. With the diver half submerged the legs are perfectly straight, with feet together and toes pointed.

17—5. The diver enters the water with a slight arch in the lower back, which is not in the best form. However, he will continue to follow the same direction and prevent an overthrow by using a reverse save technique.

17—6. Nearing the water, the body is perfectly straight, and nearly perpendicular to the water's surface. The arms are within a few degrees of perfect alignment with the whole body before contact with the water is made.

5–1. The diver starts toward the third step placement. (Note slight lean forward in preparation for longer step before the hurdle.)

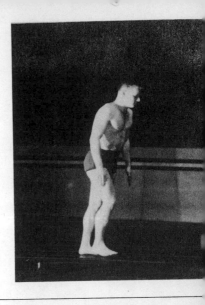

5–2. The diver is about to start his press away from the board. His heels have made a very light contact with the board, and his arms are starting up. (Notice the vertical balance that he maintains at this point in the dive.)

5–3. Arms and feet are at the highest point before starting downward for the press.

16—4. The arms are nearing a point directly over the diver's head and the arch in the back is disappearing as contact with the water is made.

16—5. Hands are now overhead and in line with the upper body as he nears the water surface, but his body has not reached the vertical as it should have.

16—6. The diver is now approaching a straight body line through the hips as the arms continue to move overhead.

6—1. The long third step is more forceful; it is this step which will determine the height he will get on the hurdle.

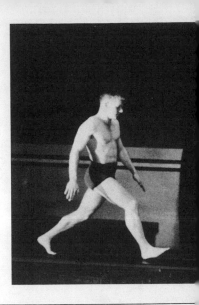

6—2. The board is now being pressed down by the diver's straightening legs and lifting arms.

6—3. A very slight bend in the knees is shown as the arms begin to lower.

15—4. The arms are being brought together overhead. The chin is moved down toward the chest to bring the head in line with the trunk. This movement will eliminate some of the arch from the back.

15—5. His hands are nearing a point of contact overhead. (Dive appears to be falling short of proper perpendicular entry.)

15—6. The legs continue to swing upward, and the diver begins to move his arms side-outward to bring them overhead in alignment with the upper body.

7—1. The diver presses down hard as he places his foot in this third step. (Notice the knee flexion, and the arms moving up to give both force and balance to the hurdle.)

7—2. The diver continues to lift his arms upward and at the same time is straightening his legs.

7—3. The knee bend is deeper and the arms continue to come down.

14—4. As the rotation continues the surface of the water comes into full view. The diver will begin to close his arms together overhead for his stretch to the water.

14—5. Diver sights point of entry into the water and begins to close arms overhead.

14—6. As the legs swing backward and upward and the upper body nears a perpendicular line to the water, the opening begins. (Notice the feet have started to move away from the hands.)

8–1. Continuing to apply force to push up into hurdle, the diver starts the left leg upward as the arms swing up.

8–2. This photo catches the diver a split second before he is pushed from the board. His arms are above his head and just a little forward. As he leaves the board, they will start down into a piking movement.

8–3. The arms have nearly reached the bottom of the downswing, and the knees are deeply flexed. (Careful examination of the previous photos will reveal that the board has remained level throughout the arm-lowering and knee-bending movement of the diver. It is not until the arms begin the upward movement that the board will bend.)

13—4. The diver drops his head backward to increase rotation and look for the water.

13—5. The diver continues to hold position while rotating over the top of the dive and beginning to drop toward the water head first.

13—6. The diver holds the pike position and the hips continue to lift; the rotation of the whole body begins as the effect of the former leg position is overpowered by the strong thrust upward of the hips and bending of the upper body forward.

9—1. The right leg pushes to near full extension; the arms are near their highest reach above the head.

9—2. The diver is thrown free of the board and has started into the pike position immediately. His legs are drawn forward to retard some of the forward rotation caused by the hip lift.

9—3. The arms are starting upward and the legs begin to straighten for the thrust. The board is bent here.

12—4. The same body position is held while the whole body rotates over the highest elevation.

12—5. As the body rotates into the horizontal plane the position of the head enables the diver to view the water from the very top of the dive.

12—6. The pike is closed as the hands are placed on the top of the insteps; the legs are still forward. (Notice that the head is held in a position which allows the diver to view the water from the very top of the lift.)

10—1. The left leg is bent at the hip joint to form a perfect right angle between the thigh and the trunk. The leg lift into this position helps the diver eliminate a forward lean of the upper body, as well as adding to the necessary force needed to gain maximum lift in the hurdle.

10—2. The action of the previous picture continues. The diver is still lifting his straight legs forward. (Notice the position of the diving board in this and photo 10—2.) Although he has started to execute the pike position, he is still moving upward.

10—3. The arms have reached upward to almost full lift, and the knees are nearly straight before leaving the board.

11—4. The arms are now in correct position in a straight line through the shoulders and head and chest are passing through the highest point in the lift. The legs continue to rise.

11—5. Continued rotation is bringing him toward the horizontal as he drops his head backward and looks for the water.

11—6. The closing of the pike is well under way as the hips continue to rise and the arms are brought down toward the feet. (Notice that the legs are still forward of a perpendicular line to the water.)

11—1. The diver is at the highest point of his hurdle in complete suspension before starting the drop to the end of the board. (Notice that he has his eyes focused on the end of the board.)

11—2. The diver has now started to bring his trunk toward his legs to close the pike.

11—3. The diver is free of the board and the arms are in full lift above the head. (Notice that there is more lean outward than there should be for a perfect takeoff.)

10—4. Immediately upon leaving the board the diver spreads his arms apart. The chest is high and the chin raised slightly. The arch is high in the upper back and not at the waist. The firmness through the waist allows the legs to climb and follow through the arch established by the head and chest.

10—5. The diver's head, shoulders, chest, and upper body pivot around a static point, while his legs continue to rise.

10—6. With the body free of the board, the piking position is begun by lifting the hips up directly from the board. To get the maximum lift from the board it is absolutely necessary that the hips be given this early strong thrust. Notice that the legs are brought forward while the hips are being raised. This retarding action by the legs is used to eliminate the excess rotation; it will not affect the lift of the dive.

12—1. The left leg begins to lower as he drops nearer to the board. The arms also begin to drop side-downward.

12—2. To close the pike, his hands are coming closer to his toes. His head is in a position which enables him to see his feet and the water while he executes the movement.

12—3. As he raises his legs from the hips, his arms are also brought forward in preparation to meet the feet at top of dive. (Note that at no time throughout the first half of the dive does the diver thrust his head backward.)

9—4. The arms reach upward to the full extension overhead while the diver's feet are in contact with the board. (Very little head tilt is noticed at this point.)

9—5. The arms are spread to a straight line through the shoulders, a position which will be held until the body rotates to a half turn.

9—6. The diver is almost clear of the board, his arms are at their highest point, and the legs have pushed to a straight line through the knees. (Notice that the diver is starting to round his upper back in preparation for the pike position.)

13-1. The arms drop to shoulder level as the legs close together.

13-2. His lift still continues as the closing is nearly complete. The legs will still be slightly forward of a perpendicular line when the hands and feet first meet.

13-3. The pike is nearly closed. To offset the fast lift of the legs caused by the excess lean from the board (photo 11-3) the hands will meet the feet before the legs are perpendicular to the water. This adjustment slows rotation and allows the diver some needed control early in the dive.

8—4. The board is pushed down to a deep bend as the arms lift upward with great force and the knees begin to straighten. (The blur in the region of the feet in this picture is caused by the tremendous speed of movement during this lifting phase.)

8—5. Almost the identical picture except that his feet have left the board, and his legs start to swing outward following the rotation started by the arms, head, and chest.

8—6. The arms reach upward again but this time slightly in front of the body, rather than in line with the sides. The legs start to straighten at the same time.

14—1. The diver is now aiming his feet directly at the end of the board, bringing his arms down forcefully so that he will be able to swing them upward to add force to the takeoff.

14—2. This picture shows a beautiful pike position with the legs straight through the knees and perfectly extended feet and pointed toes.

14—3. The pike is completely closed as the diver lays his hands on the top of his insteps.

7—4. The knees are at maximum flexion as the arms reach nearly the bottom of their swing.

7—5. This is the instant before the diver's feet lose contact with the board. He has stretched his arms above his head, and his knees are completely extended. His head is lifted, and his chest begins to follow his head lift.

7—6. The downward armswing and the knee bending is complete.

15—1. The diver has landed on the board and his heels are about to make contact. His arms are at the bottom of their downward swing and the knees are bent as he prepares to press the board into a deep bend.

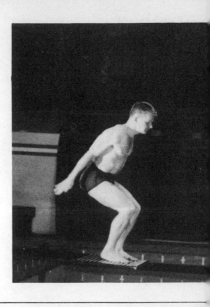

15—2. The diver holds the position while the whole body rotates enough to place his upper body perpendicular to the water.

15—3. He holds the closed pike position as his legs rise nearer to a vertical line.

6—4. The swing downward continues as the knees bend. Notice the side-downward path of the arms.

6—5. Riding the board down to a complete press, he begins to push his legs toward full extension as his arms lift upward overhead into the dive. (Note the bend in the board and the angle of the diver's body to the water. It would appear that the diver would be thrown outward a great distance from the board, but by riding the board through the complete bending and lifting phase, he will be perpendicular to the water when he leaves the board.)

6—6. As the arms are brought down the knees bend. (Notice that the arms travel downward in line with the sides of the body. This type of movement eliminates the possibility of leaning backward from the board while working it.)

16—1. The legs begin to straighten and the arms swing upward in front of the body to depress the board. Notice the slight bend of the elbows. (The diver's feet are back from the end of the board here. This placement is an error.)

16—2. Having reached the proper position, he starts his opening. Using the muscles of his lower back and buttocks, he sweeps his legs up toward alignment with his trunk.

16—3. When the legs are perpendicular to the water, the diver opens the pike with a drop backward of the head, arms, and upper body. Notice the arm action is toward the sides rather than a swinging motion directly overhead. This is another means of slowing the rotation.

5—4. Arms and heels are at maximum elevation, and the start downward follows immediately. It is at this point that the crow hop (see p. 25) is made if the arm and heel lift is too strong and not coordinated with the action of the board.

5—5. The arms are completely down at the sides and the heels in light contact with the board. (Notice the diver is in perfect balance, with his shoulders directly over his feet.)

5—6. At the top of the arm lift, the feet have pressed up high on the toes. At this point the arms will start downward.

17—1. The diver is almost to full extension. Lifting the arms as the legs straighten forces the board downward to a greater depth.

17—2. The diver continues the leg lift and starts his arms forward to a point above his head. (Notice his head position offers a chance to view the water during this entire opening phase.)

17—3. The arms continue in the same outward movement and the diver's head is back far enough for him to see the water.

4—4. The arms continue to lift upward and the diver's heels also begin to lift.

4—5. Contact has been made with the board, the diver's weight resting on the balls of the feet, and the arms continue downward. The knees are flexing in preparation for the spring from the board.

4—6. The arms continue to rise, and now the heels are being lifted.

18—1. Because he intends to return to the board after the complete press, the diver raises his head slightly just before being thrust from the board.

18—2. His body is now perfectly straight, as his arms near the proper position overhead.

18—3. The body is completely straight and the hands nearly together overhead for a perfectly aligned entry.

3—4. The diver has dropped his heels (he is using the four-movement technique) and started to lift his arms side-upward to put the board in motion. Notice the bend in the board as the arms begin to rise.

3—5. Legs are extended with feet together as he nears the board with his feet, and the arms begin the downswing.

3—6. The heels drop, followed immediately by an upward movement of the arms made outward from the sides.

19–1. He straightens his whole body, lifts his head, and carries through to a complete lift of the arms overhead.

19–2. The whole body is stretched arrow-like to the surface of the water. He has dropped his head down between his arms to achieve perfect alignment.

19–3. As contact with the water is made, his head is pulled in between his arms. This head move helps flatten the back and remove any arch that might appear.

2—4. The arms are lowered to the sides and for a brief moment the diver holds this position. (Notice that the diver is still high on his toes.)

2—5. Dropping nearer to the board he brings his legs together in preparation for his landing on the board with simultaneous placement of the feet.

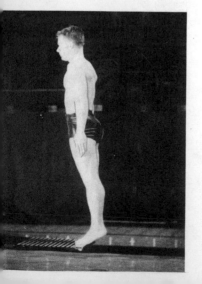

2—6. He lowers his arms to the sides, then pauses for a brief moment.

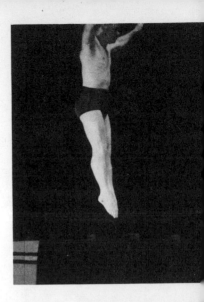

20—1. The diver has been pushed about 4 feet above the board and will return to it. His arms are held straight out from the shoulders to give balance during the drop. Before landing, he will lower his head and focus his eyes on the spot where he will land. After striking the board with his feet, he will stop his movements so as not to continue to bounce.

20—2. The diver is shown cutting through the water toward the bottom of the pool. His perfectly pointed toes are still visible above the water.

20—3. The entry is nearly complete. Notice perfect feet and continued stretch toward bottom of pool. When dives have this vertical drop into the water with very little rotation, the diver will try to hold the angle of entry until the feet disappear below the surface of the water.

4. Back Dive (Layout)

1—4. The diver stands in a balanced position with his arms straight ahead at shoulder level. Notice that the hands are held in a straight line with the forearms. Some divers neglect this somewhat minor detail and have the hand pointing up or down from the wrist.

5. Reverse Dive (Layout)

1—5. The diver is shown at the moment he begins the descent to the board from a high hurdle. (Note that he is looking down directly at the board.)

6. Inward Dive (Pike)

1—6. The diver is standing in the proper position to begin with the four-movement technique: heels raised and arms held straight forward from the shoulders, parallel with the board. From this position his heels will drop to start the board in motion.

4. Back Dive (Layout)

---

5. Reverse Dive (Layout)

---

6. Inward Dive (Pike)

7. Forward Dive
One-half Twist (Layout)

―――――――

8. Forward One-and-one-half
Somersault (Pike)

―――――――

9. Inward One-and-one-half
Somersault (Tuck)

7. Forward Dive One-half Twist (Layout)

1–7. This picture shows the diver in the step before his hurdle. (Notice the heel–toe placement of the right foot.)

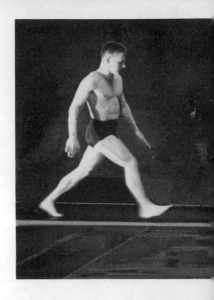

8. Forward One-and-one-half Somersault

1–8. Reaching high above his head and lifting his free leg up to form a perfect right angle with his trunk, the diver eyes the end of the board for placement of his feet as he hurdles toward it.

9. Inward One-and-one-half Somersault (Tuck)

1–9. Proper standing position for a backward standing dive. (Note: The success you achieve in performing the inward spinning dives is almost entirely dependent upon your board work during the takeoff. The first ten pictures in this series pertain to this phase of the dive. The crucial points and proper techniques are clearly shown.)

20—10. With only the feet above the water, the diver has almost completely remedied the early error and presents a good entry.

20—11. The minimum of splash proves the perfection of the entry.

20—12. The diver slides cleanly into the water. Notice the perfect leg and toe position.

2—7. The lift into the hurdle shows perfect position of the pressing leg as well as the lifting leg. (Notice the right angle formed by the thigh and upper body.)

2—8. His arms begin to be lowered toward his sides and his legs come together during the descent to the board.

2—9. The diver has lowered his arms to his sides, where he pauses momentarily. Most divers use this pause as an adjustment period for balance and a mental preparation for the dive.

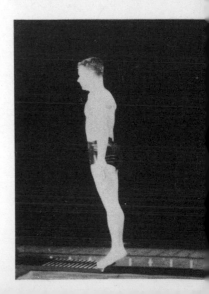

19—10. Although almost completely submerged, he continues to arch his back in a reverse save. The action has helped. Evidence: the new angle of entry at which the lower legs have arrived.

19—11. The point of the feet and toes here is excellent.

19—12. The opening is nearly complete as he stretches his arms overhead and assumes a proper angle of entry.

3—7. The drop to the board begins with the closing of the legs and lowering of the arms. (Note: The diver is looking at the end of the board.)

3—8. Falling in a perfectly straight line from head to toes, the diver continues to look at the end of the board carefully. It is at this point in the approach that you are apt to make the common error of bending forward at the waist.

3—9. The diver has started the board in motion and is in the process of lifting his arms up. He is also about to lift his heels.

18—10. The diver resorts to a back arching movement to bring the body to a better angle of entry.

18—11. A clean entry into the water with head and arms has been made, and the legs are in perfect position.

18—12. Moving his arms overhead, he lifts his legs up behind and the opening continues.

4—7. As the diver continues to drop nearer to the board, his legs come together. However, the most important point to observe is the arm position. Notice that the arms are being lowered side-downward and are not at any time behind the body.

4—8. With only a few inches left before the diver touches the board with his feet, the knees show a bending action.

4—9. This is the completion of the second movement of a four-movement takeoff technique. The diver's arms have been raised side-upward and are in perfect position for this dive, i.e., slightly forward of his head.

17—10. With his body completely straight and his arms overhead, he descends to the water. The earlier mistake in judgment shows up in the angle of the body with the water.

17—11. The diver continues the stretch to the water.

17—12. The pike is opening as the diver picks the spot in the water where he plans to enter.

5—7. The drop continues. (Notice the pointed toes. The diver naturally must flatten the feet as they strike the board, but during the drop they must be pointed to give the controlled effect.)

5—8. Contact with the board is made as the diver lands on the balls of his feet. (Note that even though the diver has dropped from a height of approximately two feet, very little bend is shown in the board. The deep bend in the board will come as the diver's arms travel upward and he straightens his legs to push away.)

5—9. The beginning of the third phase in the takeoff is shown here. The arms are coming down to the sides as the diver bends his knees. The important point in this movement is to keep perfect balance and not allow the body to lean back away from a perpendicular line to the board. The balance is controlled by keeping the hips directly above the feet and the shoulders in the same plane.

16–10. Aware at this point that he is not in a good position for a vertical drop to the water, he makes an adjustment in his arm movement. If the kickout had been made at the proper time, he would have brought his arms overhead with a side-outward movement. However, to continue the rotation, he swings them with force directly in front of his face into position overhead.

16–11. The arms are now stretched above his head in final position. (Notice that the head is brought forward for good alignment of the whole body for the entry.)

16–12. The rotation is now far enough into the last half-somersault for the diver to see the water and prepare for the entry.

6—7. The diver is about to land on the board. He will strike the board with the balls of his feet before allowing the heels to come in contact with it.

6—8. The heels drop to the board and the knees continue to bend deeper. The diver's arms have reached the low point in their swing. From this point on, the board and diver must be in perfect rhythm to ensure maximum thrust upward.

6—9. At the end of the third movement, the diver is shown in a deep knee bend. His arms are about to swing upward. (Notice that the arms are bent at the elbows and kept from extending behind the hips.)

15—10. The legs are nearly straight through the knees before any action with the arms is noticeable. The diver is looking backward to see the water.

15—11. The diver's body is completely extended and he is looking directly at the water.

15—12. He continues rotation after stopping the twist.

7—7. Contact is made, and the knees begin to flex in preparation for pressing the board downward.

7—8. With his arms lifting upward in front of his face, he straightens his legs, pushing the board down to its greatest depth.

7—9. The board has been pushed down to its maximum bend and is recovering upward as the diver straightens his legs and lifts his arms in front of his face.

14–10. The diver continues to extend his legs, causing the hands to release their grip on the legs.

14–11. The arms start to move to a position overhead as the whole body is extending to a straight layout position. Because the diver has selected the correct time for his kickout, his arm will swing overhead with a lateral movement.

14–12. The diver moves his arms down to deepen the pike and eliminate the twisting action.

8—7. The diver's arms have reached their lowest point as his legs start to straighten for his dive from the board.

8—8. While still in contact with the board, the diver rounds his back as he anticipates the movements into a forward spin. Before he leaves the board he will bend slightly at the waist.

8—9. The arms have reached their highest point and have started downward before the legs have been completely extended. This action indicates that he will start his spin and tucking action directly from the board.

13—10. This is the first indication that the diver is about to extend his body for the opening. He has loosened his hold on his legs and his lower leg is starting to align with his thigh. He has also started to throw his head back to look for the water. But the diver has opened too early in the spin, an error which will be noticeable in succeeding pictures.

13—11. The head is now well back as the diver looks for the water. (It is necessary to see the water before adjusting the arms overhead for entry.)

13—12. This photo is about the same as the preceding one but shows an advanced position in twisting and somersaulting.

9—7. The arms lift upward in front of the chest with some bend at the elbows. (Notice the deep bend in the board at this point.)

9—8. Free from the board, he is already in the complete pike position, but he will continue to rise as he spins.

9—9. The arms, head, and upper body have begun to move downward toward a tuck position, to be completed as soon as the feet are free of the board and the hip lift has started.

12–10. The diver has completed one full somersault. Although his feet are not pointed to an extreme extension, they are in fairly good position. Quite often a diver will flex the ankles while doing a reverse spin and present an awkward foot.

12–11. The kickout continues. The arms begin to move to an overhead position and the diver is shown in a definite pike position.

12–12. Still twisting toward the full twist, the pike position is deepened to help the somersaulting force.

10—7. The spreading of the arms has begun, even before the feet are free from the board. The diver has already initiated the twisting force.

10—8. The diver has rotated one-half turn in a perfect pike position. His hips have reached a high point and will remain at this point while his legs and upper body pivot around them.

10—9. Notice the hips are pushed up and the legs have started to bend at the knees, a movement which will bring the heels up toward the buttocks and create additional force for forward rotation.

11—10. Spinning in a good tuck position, the diver is nearing one full somersault. Careful examination of the pictures will show that throughout the entire spin to this point he has continued to gain elevation.

11—11. The kickout to slow the rotation starts. The first movement is made by the legs as they are straightened at the knees. Notice the diver is raising his chin and begins to move his head backward. This is the first action of the head in the execution of a reverse spinning dive.

11—12. As the diver passes three-quarters of a full twist, he begins to bend to a pike position.

11—7. Flying upward, the arms are set to perfect alignment (spread to a straight line through the shoulders). The legs begin to rise up behind. This is the same movement that is used in the Forward Dive (Layout).

11—8. Nearing three-quarters of a turn, the diver holds the same perfect position.

11—9. The tuck is beginning to take shape, but it is not quite as tight as it should be at this point.

10–10. The diver rotates in a tight tuck position without any obvious head thrust or back arch. Careful examination of photos 5–10 through 9–10 should be convincing proof that the spin is created by lifting the knees to the chest as soon as the feet leave the board. The arms must be swung upward above the head during the takeoff, but arching the back and thrusting the head back is not only unnecessary but fundamentally wrong.

10–11. Notice that the head has still not been thrown back as the diver nears one complete turn.

10–12. The body has twisted one-half turn and has completed one-half somersault. The arms are now in proper twisting position.

12—7. The rotation of the whole body continues and the twist is blending into the swan or front dive position. The action of the arms is the key to the twisting. The head is held with chin up slightly, but the diver has his eyes fixed on the water.

12—8. The diver continues his rotation as he waits to reach a point where he can see the water while still high above it and can prepare for the opening phase of the dive.

12—9. The diver has gathered into a compact tuck position and at the same time continues to rotate and rise higher above the board.

9—10. The tuck is compact and complete by the time he has turned one-half somersault. (The hands should be slightly lower on the legs than shown here.)

9—11. The rotation continues to the top of the spin.

9—12. The body can be seen twisting to the left as the pike opens and the arms move toward their complete twisting position.

13—7. The legs continue to climb and, as they approach the horizontal line to the water, the twist is nearly one-quarter of a full turn, or half completed.

13—8. One complete somersault is finished and the diver is still in a beautiful deep pike position with his arms straight in a line through the shoulders. His legs are held firmly together and his feet and toes pointed to a perfect taper.

13—9. Passing through a complete somersault, he is in a tight tuck position and is pivoting around the highest point in his lift.

8—10. This picture clearly demonstrates the theory that the quick gather into the tuck position is correct. By the time he has turned one-quarter somersault he is in a fairly tight tuck position.

8—11. Hands holding firmly to the upper shins, the arms pull in to tighten the tuck position as rotation continues.

8—12. This photo shows the diver changing the position of his arms. He has started to swing his right arm across his chest and his left arm above his head. This action causes a twist to the left. As this twist is started, the diver will open the pike. (It is necessary to be in a straight body position to twist fast and in balance.)

14—7. With the body parallel to the water, the twist is passing into the final one-quarter turn and will be completed as the descent to the water is made.

14—8. Holding a similar position, his body rotates one-quarter turn more. At this point the diver can see the water and can begin to open for his stretch.

14—9. The diver has turned one-and-one-quarter times and is beginning to open for his entry.

7—10. The tuck is started immediately by bringing the knees up toward the chest. The arms are coming down so he can grasp his shins and pull to a tight tuck position.

7—11. The diver gathers early into the tuck; note that he has rotated barely one-quarter somersault. The tuck is not yet quite complete, but it will be as he pulls in tighter with the arms.

7—12. The diver has been thrown clear of the board and is starting into his pike position. The movement must be made by a strong hip lift. The force from this early lift must be enough to carry him through the one-and-one-half somersault.

15—7. The diver's head is starting to lead the whole body downward to the water as the legs continue to rise.

15—8. The diver starts to align his legs with the upper body. This movement is made by using the large muscles of the buttocks and lower back group.

15—9. He continues to open the tuck toward full extension.

6—10. The diver has straightened his legs and his arms have reached high above his head. Again notice the good head position and the absence of an arch in the back.

6—11. He is well above the board here, and his arms start to come down to meet his legs as the tuck is begun by the hip and knee flexion. Notice his head position; it is not necessary to thrust the head back vigorously to create a reverse or backward spin.

6—12. The action continues as he prepares to leave the board. The arms are about to move downward.

16—7. The body is nearing the completion of one-half turn. The diver can now observe the exact spot at which he will enter the water. Although this position resembles a back dive, it will feel very much like a forward header from this point on.

16—8. As the opening continues the arms are being brought overhead toward a position in line with the trunk.

16—9. The diver is now nearing full extension; all that remains is to align his arms with his upper body as he reaches for the water.

5—10. The board is pressed down by the force exerted against it by his straightening legs and lifting arms. There is a little lifting of the chin, which is a recommended technique at this point in the dive, but it is important to note that the diver has not thrown his head back to initiate the spin.

5—11. The diver's arms are well above his head but not reaching backward. This action is correct. However, the diver is not in perfect position as he leaves the board due to a slight lean forward during the press. (That is, his hips are quite clearly forward of the end of the board—and this error could make the dive more difficult.)

5—12. His arms are swinging up above his head before he leaves the board.

17—7. The twist practically complete, the arms are being brought together overhead.

17—8. The diver has selected the point of entry and continues to open the pike for perfect alignment before striking the water with his hands.

17—9. The extension is now complete except for closing the hands together.

4–10. The end of the third movement finds him in a deep knee bend. His arms are passing from a downward swing toward the lifting phase.

4–11. This picture shows the diver at the bottom of his press. His arms are reaching upward in front of his face as his legs press hard against the board. (The most important clue shown here for proper execution of this dive is the head and upper back position. Notice that the head is not thrown backward and that the upper back is not arched.)

4–12. The diver lands on the balls of his feet and continues to bend his knees deeper, as his arms start upward.

18—7. The arms continue to close overhead.

18—8. Half submerged, he stretches his legs and toes to give a final appearance of perfection and cleanness to the entry.

18—9. The diver passes into the water. (Note that the toes are not quite together as they should be.)

3—10. This photo catches him at the top of his second move in oscillating the board.

3—11. Contact is made with the board and the bend of the knees increases. His arms are starting their upswing into the lifting stage of the dive. (Notice the bend in the arms at the elbow; this is a correct technique.)

3—12. He has started to bend his knees before actual contact with the board in order to press it to its maximum depth.

19—7. With hands clasped together, the diver enters the water. (Notice the arms are held straight and tight to the sides of his head.)

19—8. He is now deep into the water. (Notice the small splash.)

19—9. He continues to descend into the water with very little splash.

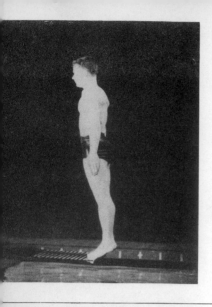

2–10. He has lowered his arms to his sides and pauses slightly before starting to put the board in motion.

2–11. Here the diver is about to land on the end of the board. His arms are coming down with great speed and his knees are bending slightly prior to contact with the board.

2–12. As the diver drops nearer the board, his arms start downward toward his sides and his legs come together.

20—7. Descending into the water cleanly, all that remains above the surface is the lower part of the legs and the beautifully pointed feet.

20—8. The diver descends toward the bottom of the pool after a nearly perfect dive.

20—9. He sinks beneath the water after a nearly perfect entry which shows a minimum of splash.

10. Back One-and-one-half Somersault (Tuck)

1—10. The diver is shown in the correct standing position for the start of all backward dives. He is in good balance, which he controls by holding his arms straight forward from the shoulders. His eyes are focused on the fixed end of the board.

11. Reverse One-and-one-half Somersault (Tuck)

1—11. The diver has made his forward approach and hurdle and this picture shows him dropping to the board. His arms are in a beautifully balanced position as he sights the end of the board for good placement of the feet.

12. Forward One-and-one-half Somersault, One Twist (Pike)

1—12. The diver starts down from a high hurdle. This photo clearly shows that the diver is looking at the end of the board as he drops.

10. Back One-and-one-half Somersault (Tuck)

---

11. Reverse One-and-one-half Somersault (Tuck)

---

12. Forward One-and-one-half Somersault, One Twist (Pike)

Index

145